FOR ORGANS, PIANOS & ELECTRONIC KEYBOARDS

E-Z PLAY TODAY

298

Beautiful Love

2ND EDITION

T0058967

ISBN 978-0-7935-3487-6

HAL•LEONARD®
CORPORATION

7777 W. BLUEMOUND RD. P.O. BOX 13819 MILWAUKEE, WI 53213

Visit Hal Leonard Online at
www.halleonard.com

(They Long to Be)
Close to You

Registration 10
Rhythm: Swing, Shuffle, or Ballad

Lyric by Hal David
Music by Burt Bacharach

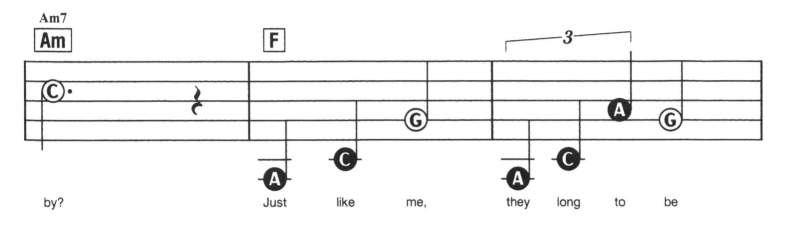

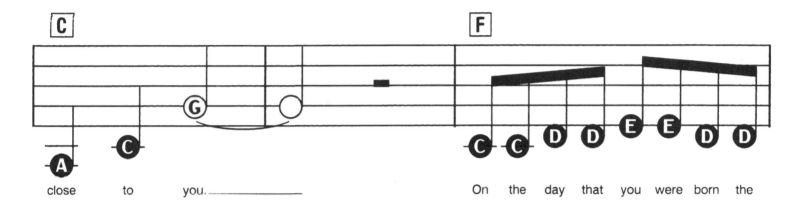

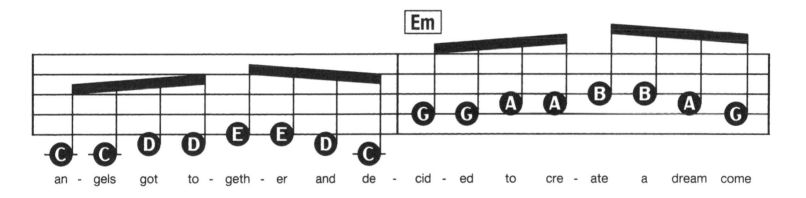

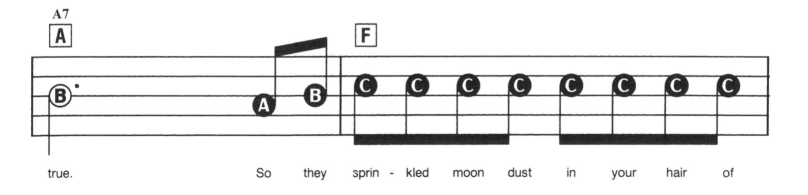

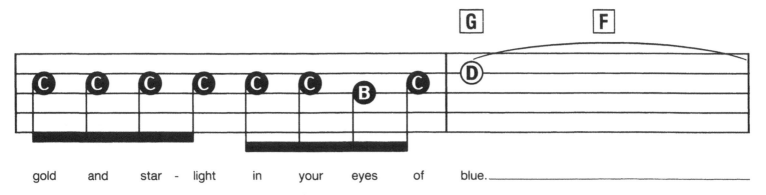

gold and star - light in your eyes of blue._____

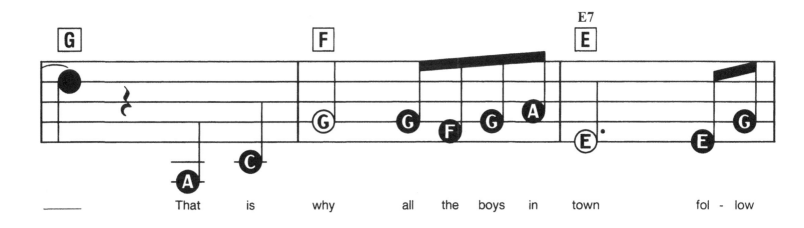

_____ That is why all the boys in town fol - low

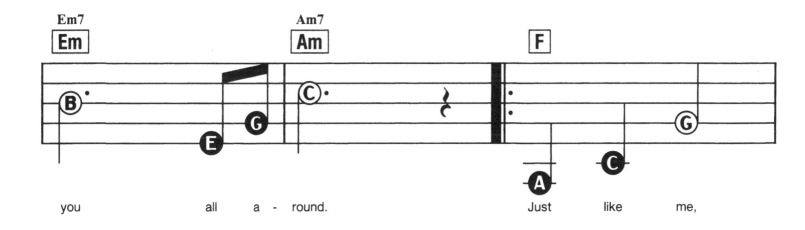

you all a - round. Just like me,

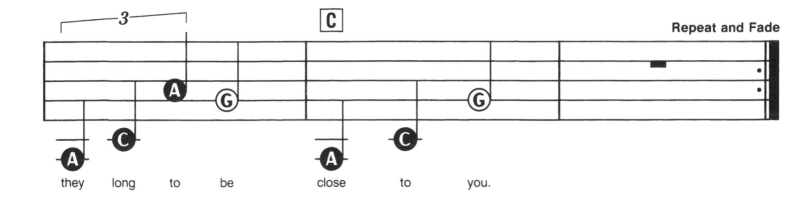

they long to be close to you.

(Everything I Do)
I Do It for You
from the Motion Picture ROBIN HOOD: PRINCE OF THIEVES

Registration 8
Rhythm: Rock or 8 Beat

Words and Music by Bryan Adams,
Robert John Lange and Michael Kamen

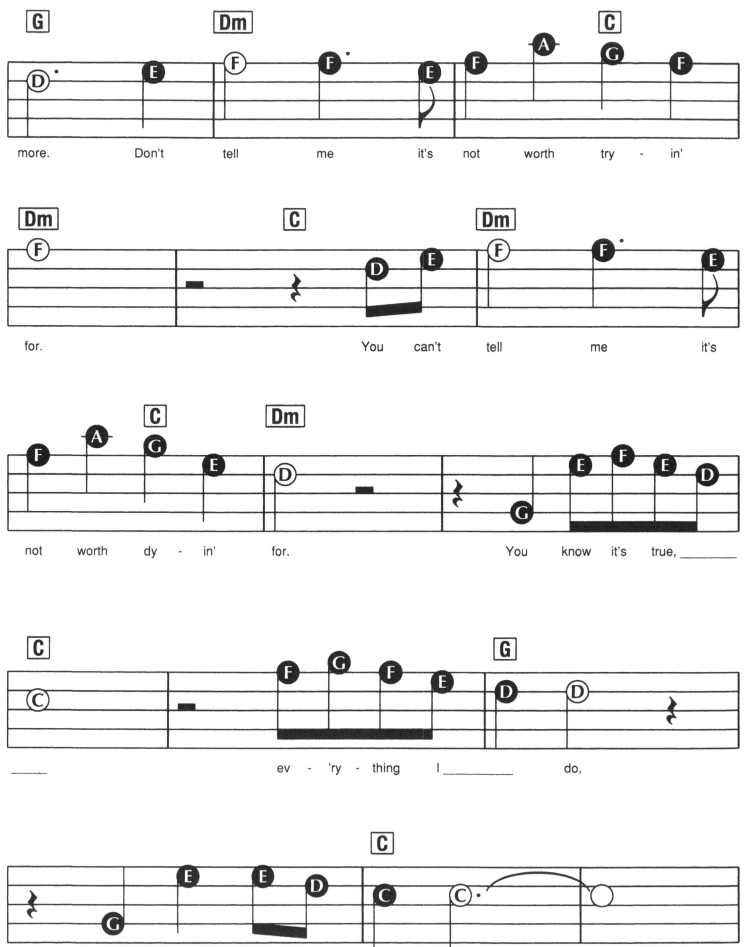

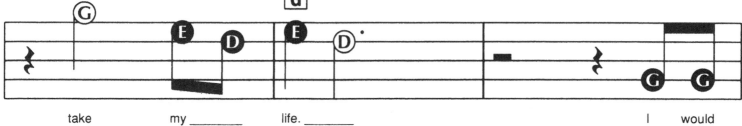

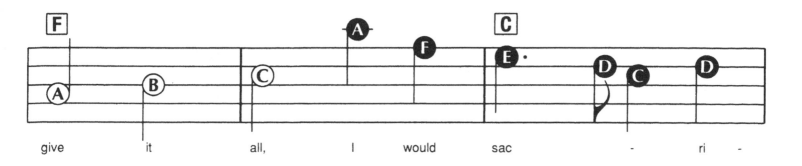

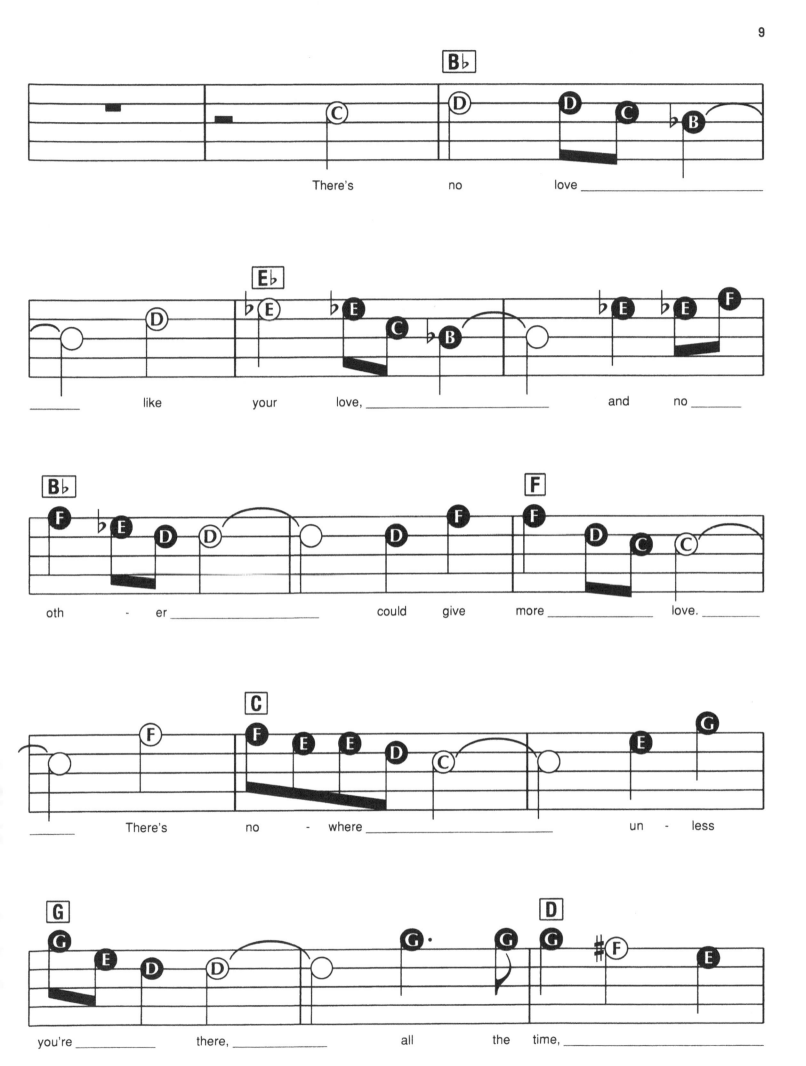

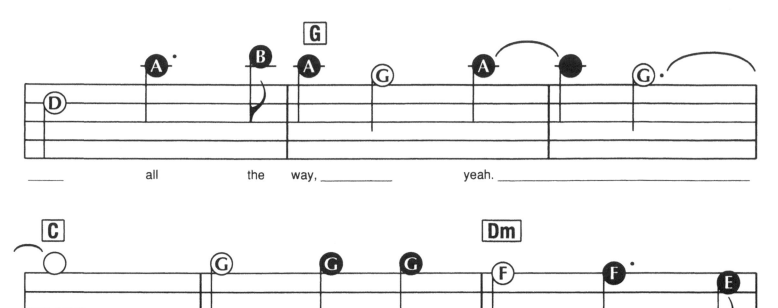

all   the   way, _____   yeah. _____

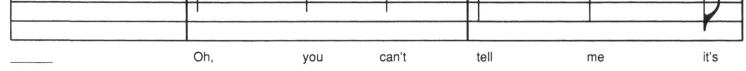

_____   Oh,   you   can't   tell   me   it's

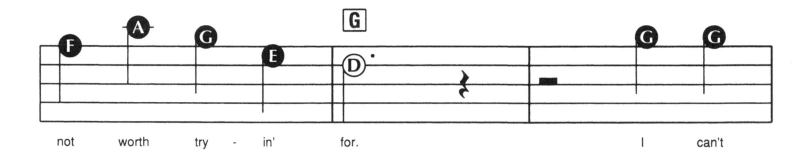

not   worth   try - in'   for.   I   can't

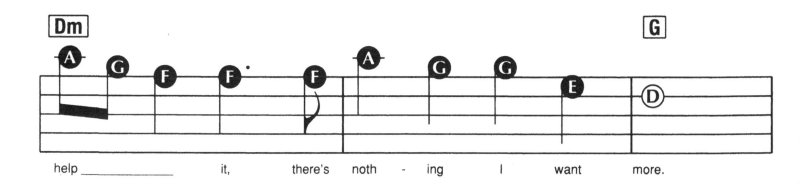

help _____   it,   there's   noth - ing   I   want   more.

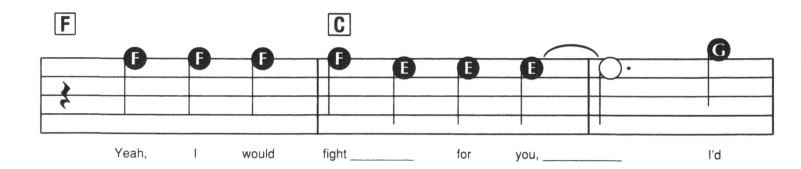

Yeah,   I   would   fight _____   for   you, _____   I'd

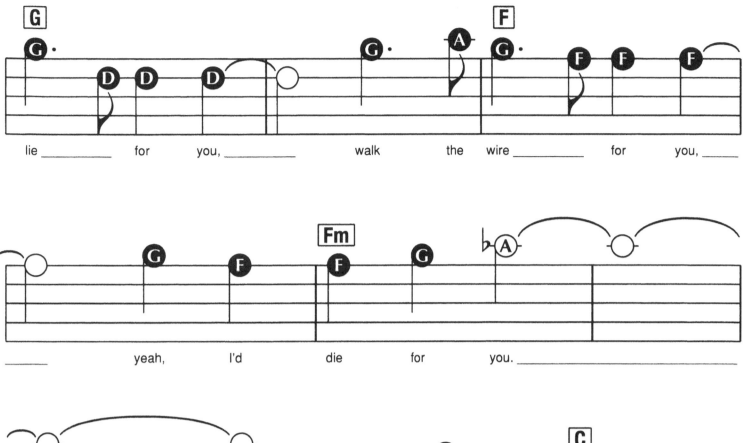

lie _____ for you, _____ walk the wire _____ for you, _____

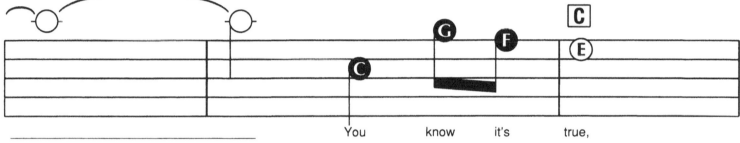

_____ yeah, I'd die for you. _____

_____ You know it's true,

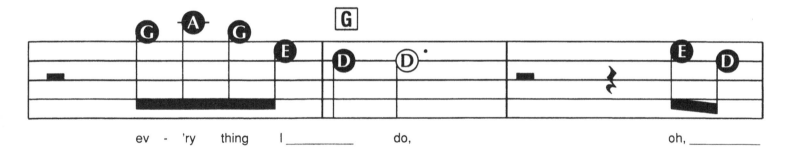

ev - 'ry thing I _____ do, oh, _____

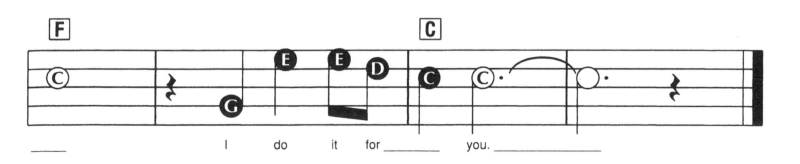

____ I do it for _____ you. _____

For Once in My Life

Registration 8
Rhythm: Rock or Pops

Words by Ronald Miller
Music by Orlando Murden

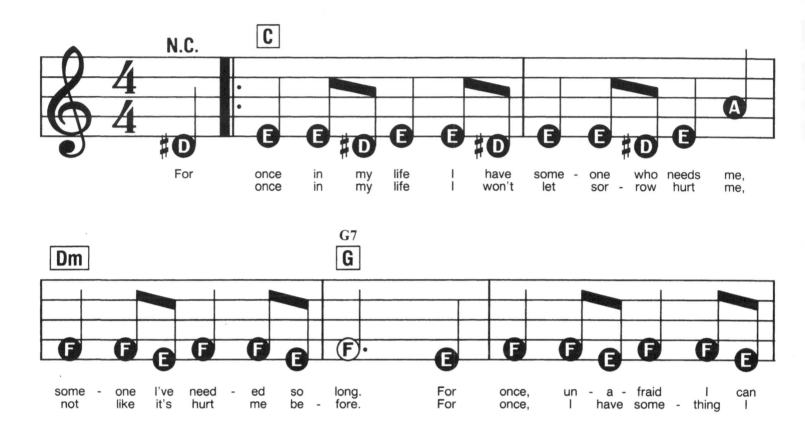

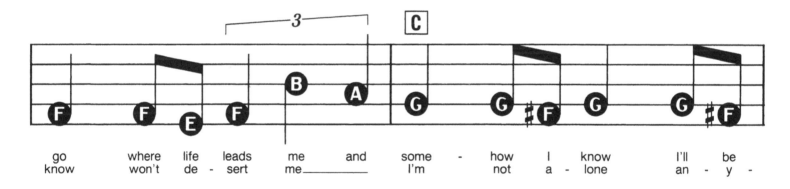

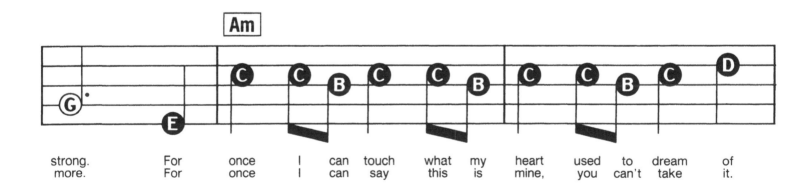

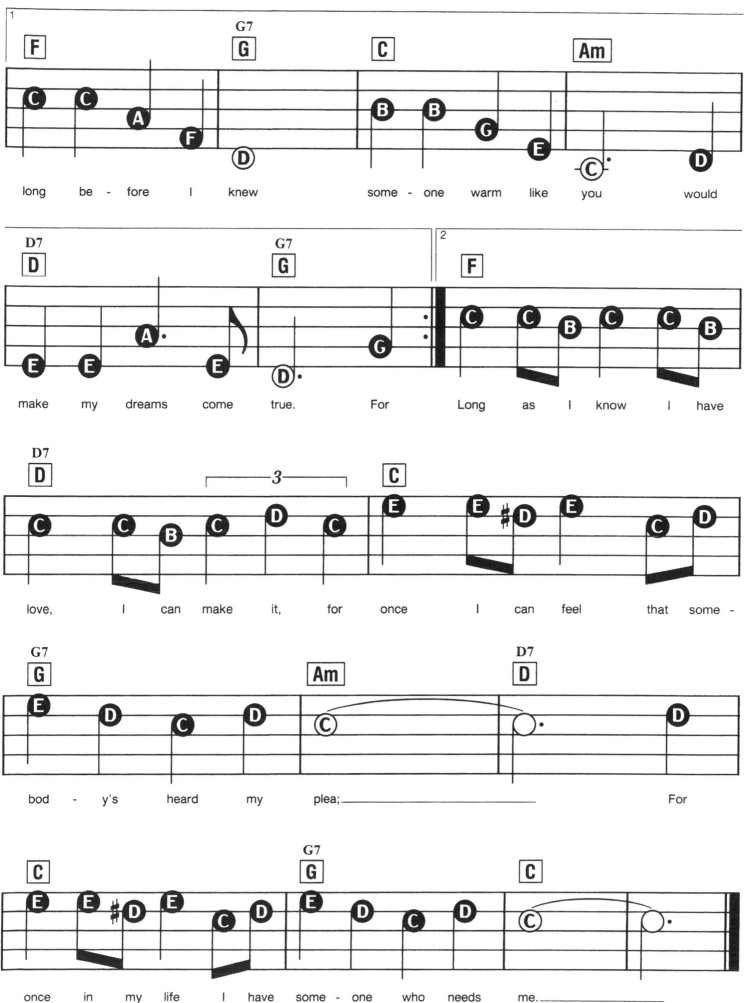

For the First Time
from ONE FINE DAY

Registration 8
Rhythm: Ballad or Pop

Words and Music by James Newton Howard,
Jud Friedman and Allan Rich

Are those your eyes? Is that your smile? I've been
real? Can this be true? Am I the

look-ing at you ___ for-ev-er, yet I nev-er saw you be-fore. Are those your
per-son I was ___ this morn-ing, and are you the same ___ you? It's all so

hands hold-ing mine? Now I won-der how I could have been so
strange. How can it be? All a - long this love was right in front of

blind.
me. } And for the first time, I am look-ing in your eyes. For the

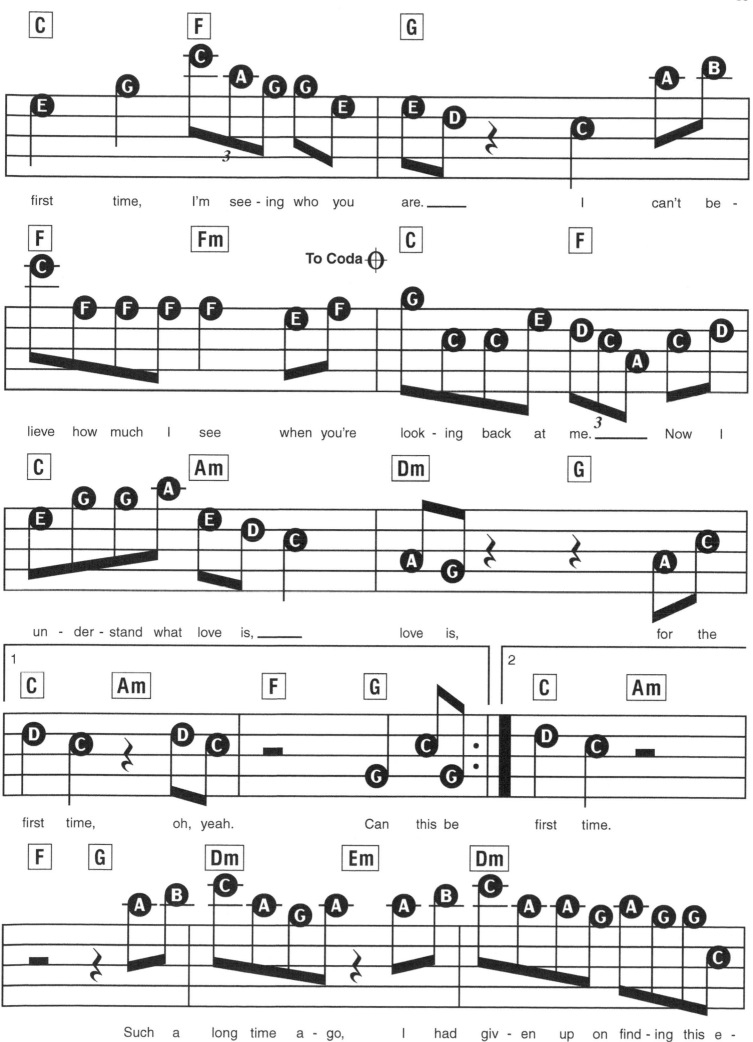

16

mo - tion   ev - er a - gain. _____   But you're

here with me now.   Yes, I   found you some-how,   and I've nev - er been so

D.S. al Coda
(Return to %
Play to ⊕ and
Skip to Coda)

CODA

sure.   And   for the   look - ing back at me. _____

Now I   un - der-stand what love is, ___   love is,   for the

first time,   for the first   time. _____

Glory of Love
Theme from KARATE KID PART II

Registration 1
Rhythm: Rock

Words and Music by David Foster,
Peter Cetera and Diane Nini

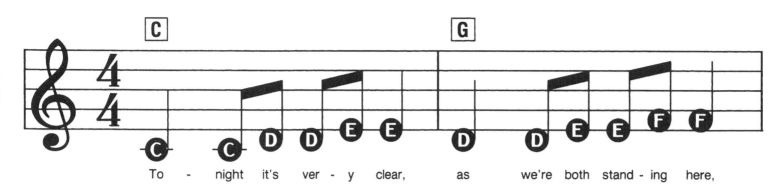

To - night it's ver - y clear, as we're both stand - ing here,

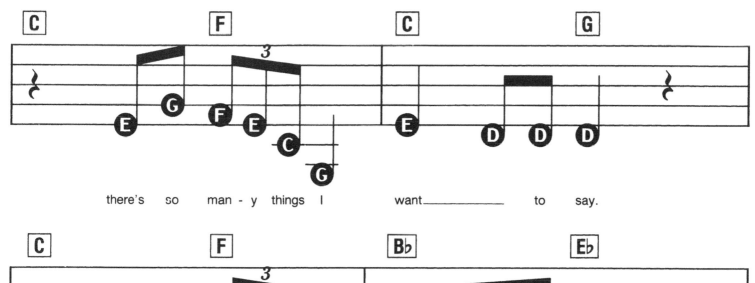

there's so man - y things I want_____ to say.

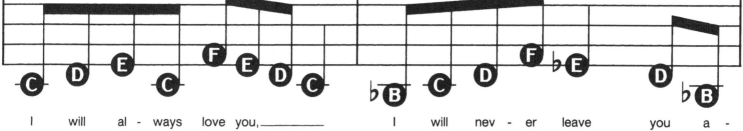

I will al - ways love you,_____ I will nev - er leave you a -

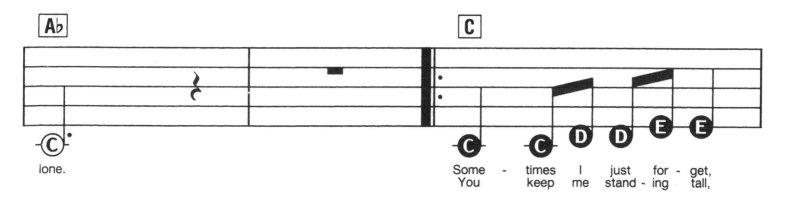

lone.

Some - times I just for - get,
You keep me stand - ing tall,

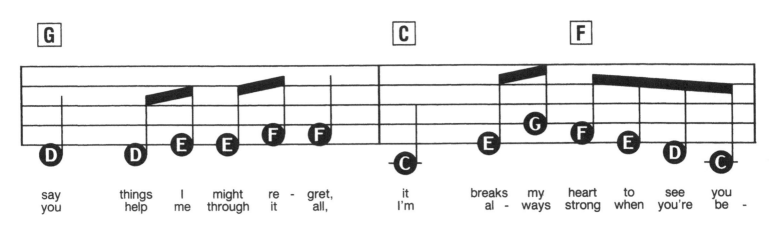

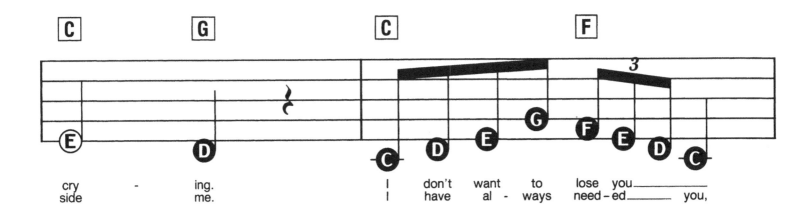

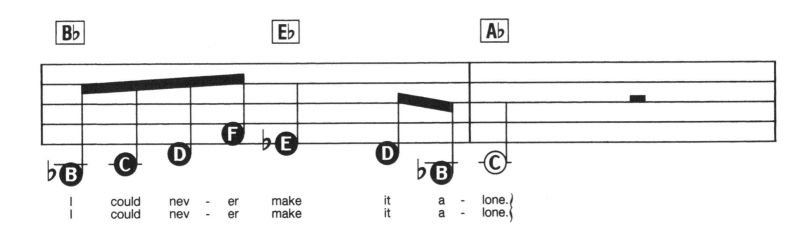

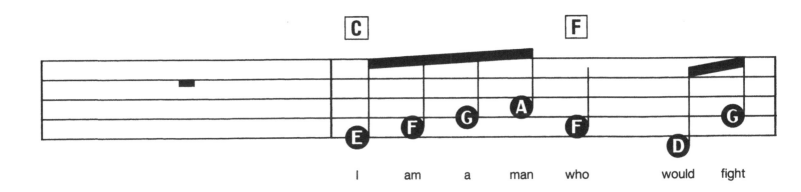

Have I Told You Lately

Registration 2
Rhythm: Rock or 8 Beat

Words and Music by
Van Morrison

Have I told you late-ly that I love you? Have I

told you there's no one else a - bove you?

Fill my heart with glad - ness, take a - way all my sad - ness,

ease my troub - les, that's what you do.

{ 1. For the
{ 2. *Instrumental*

23

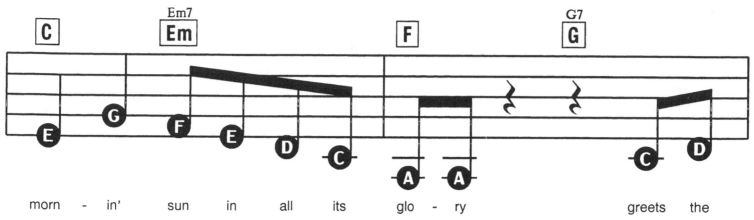

morn - in' sun in all its glo - ry greets the

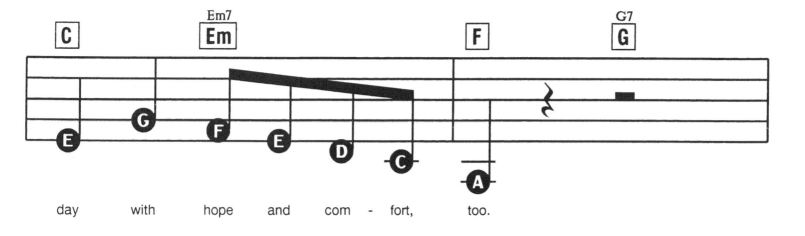

day with hope and com - fort, too.

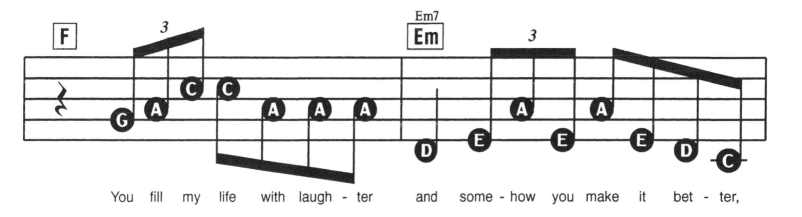

You fill my life with laugh - ter and some - how you make it bet - ter,

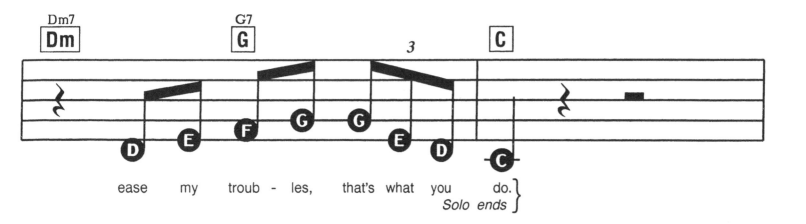

ease my troub - les, that's what you do.
Solo ends

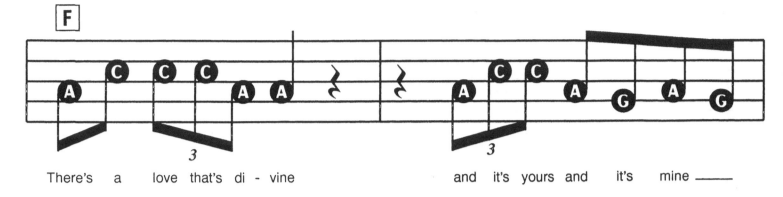

There's a love that's di - vine and it's yours and it's mine ____

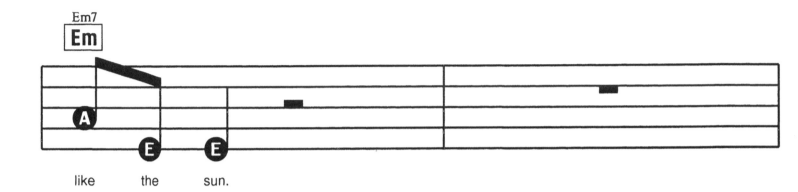

like the sun.

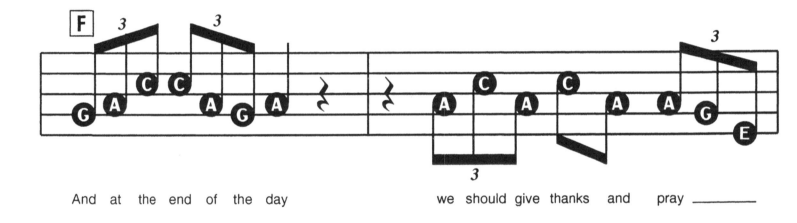

And at the end of the day we should give thanks and pray _____

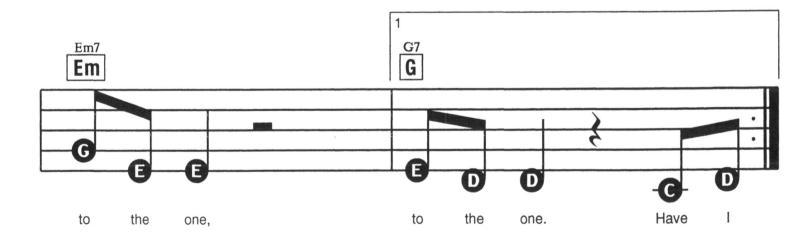

to the one, to the one. Have I

25

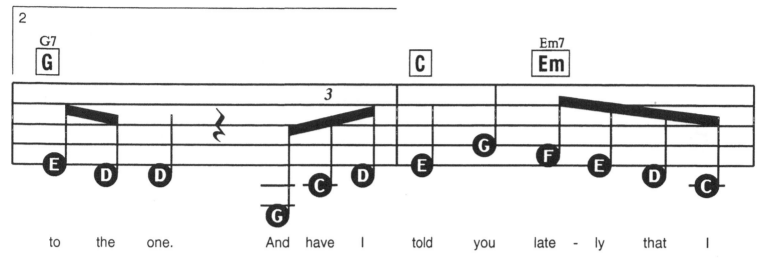

to the one. And have I told you late - ly that I

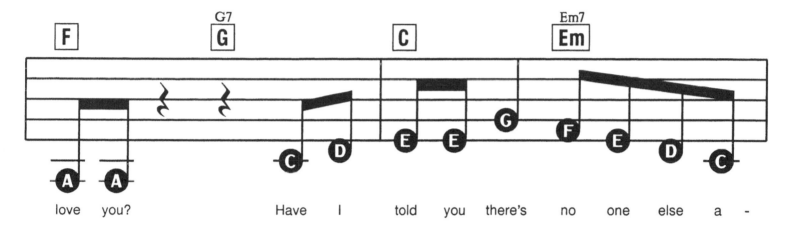

love you? Have I told you there's no one else a -

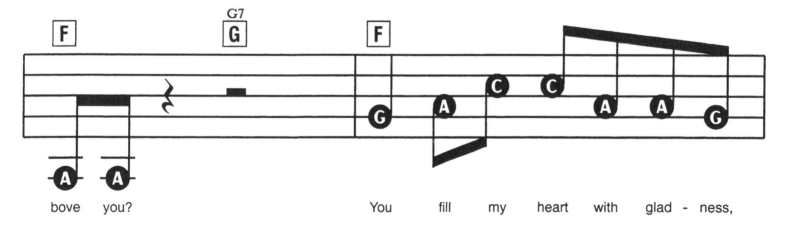

bove you? You fill my heart with glad - ness,

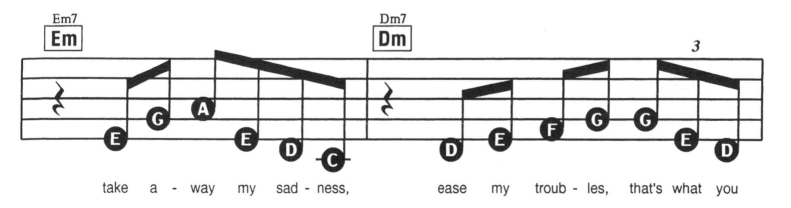

take a - way my sad - ness, ease my troub - les, that's what you

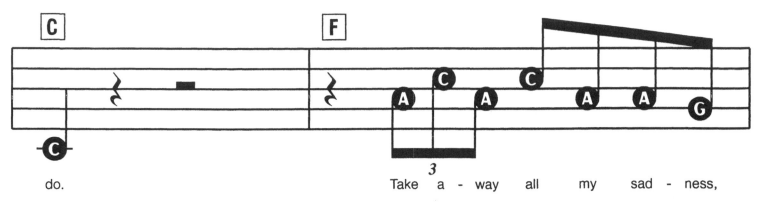

do.　　Take a - way all my sad - ness,

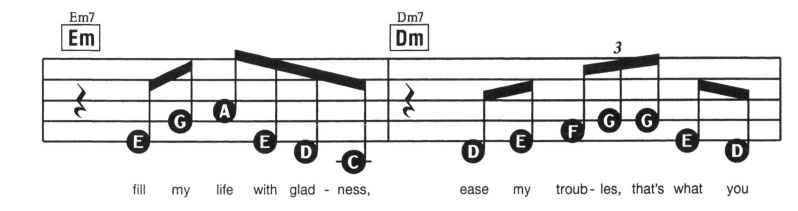

fill my life with glad - ness,　　ease my troub - les, that's what you

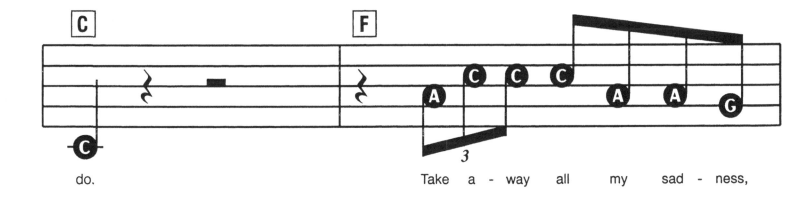

do.　　Take a - way all my sad - ness,

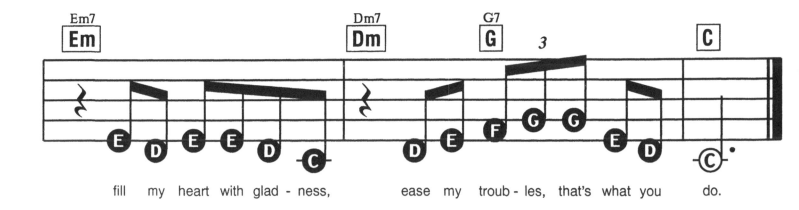

fill my heart with glad - ness,　　ease my troub - les, that's what you do.

Here and Now

Registration 8
Rhythm: 16 Beat, 8 Beat, or Rock

Words and Music by Terry Steele
and David Elliot

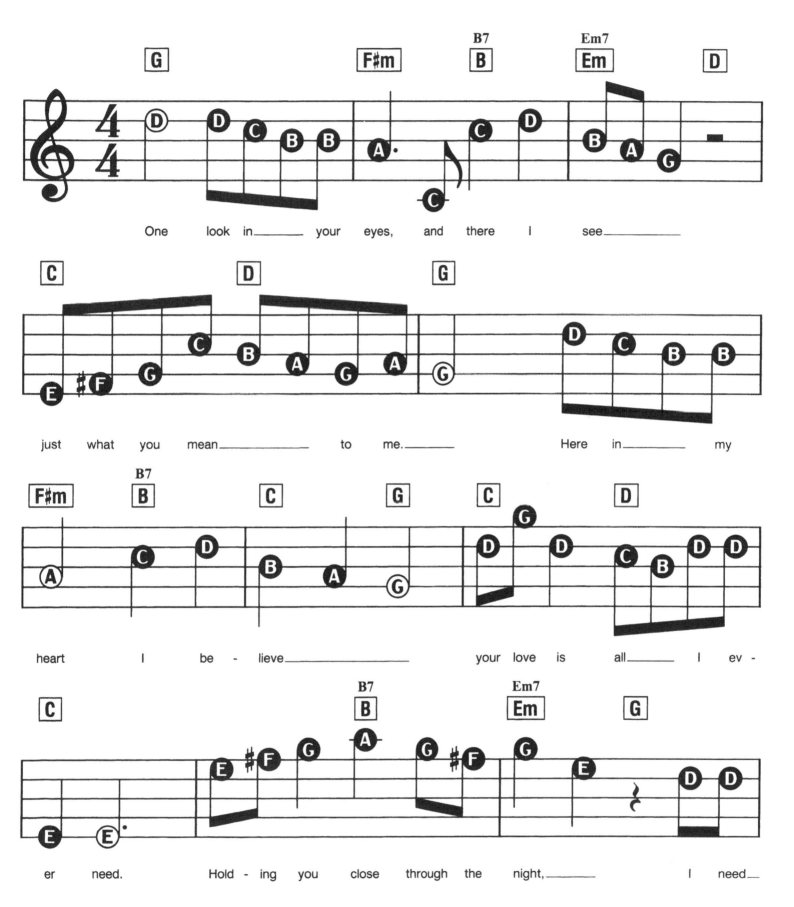

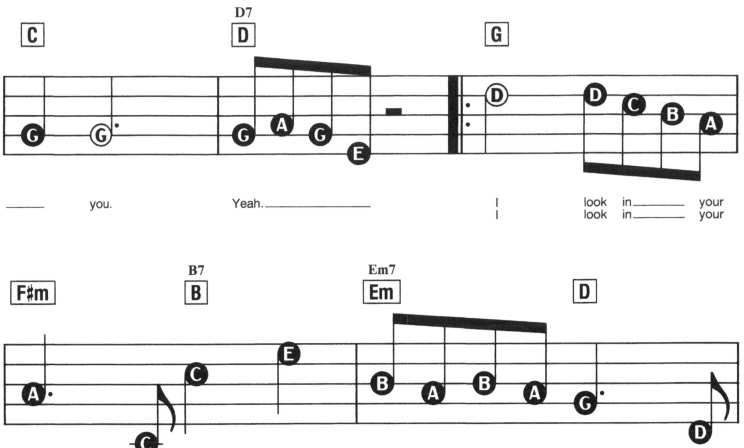

you.   Yeah._____   I   look in_____ your

I   look in_____ your

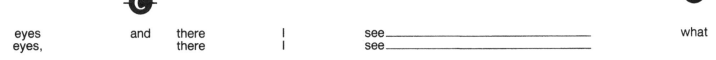

eyes,   and   there   I   see_____   what

eyes,   there   I   see_____

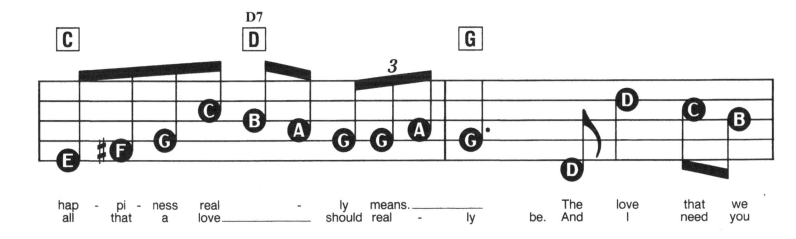

hap - pi - ness real   - ly means._____ The love that we

all that a love_____ should real - ly be. And I need you

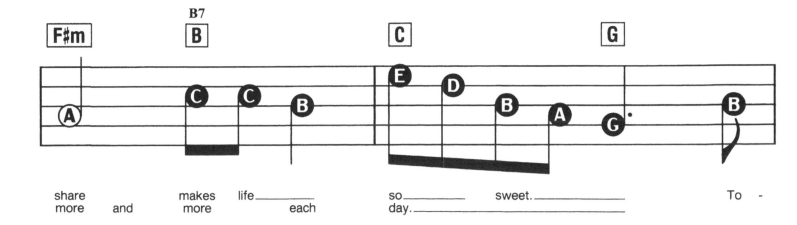

share   makes life_____ so_____ sweet._____ To -

more and   more   each   day._____

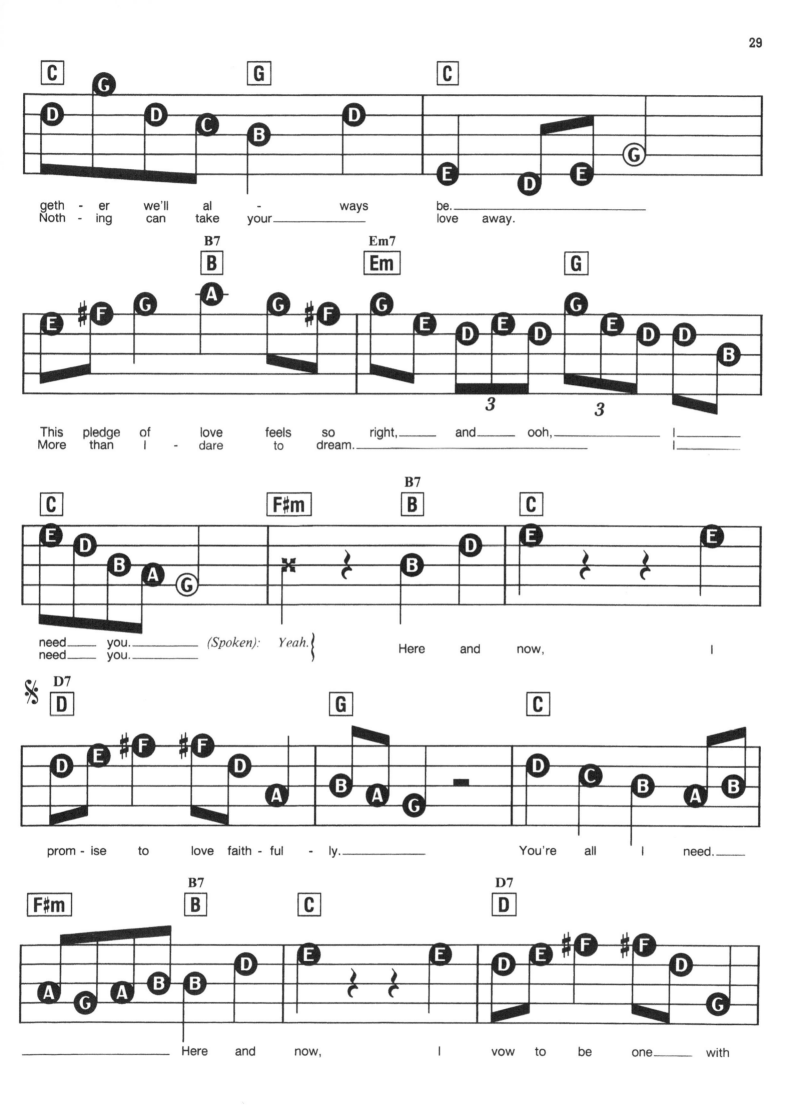

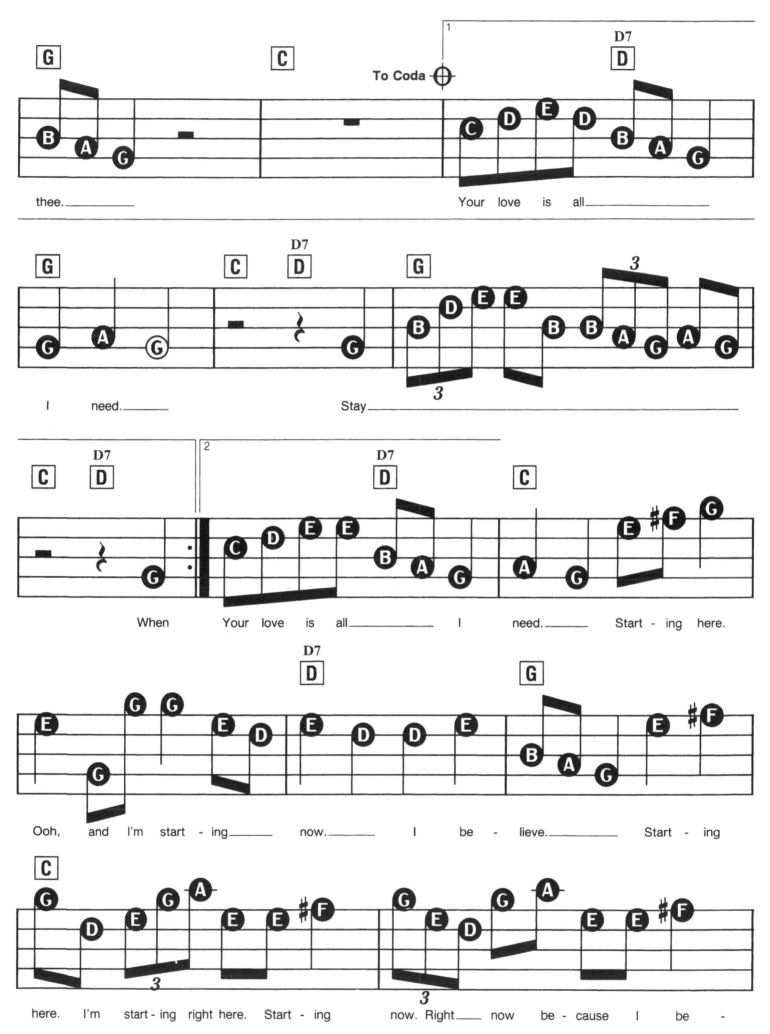

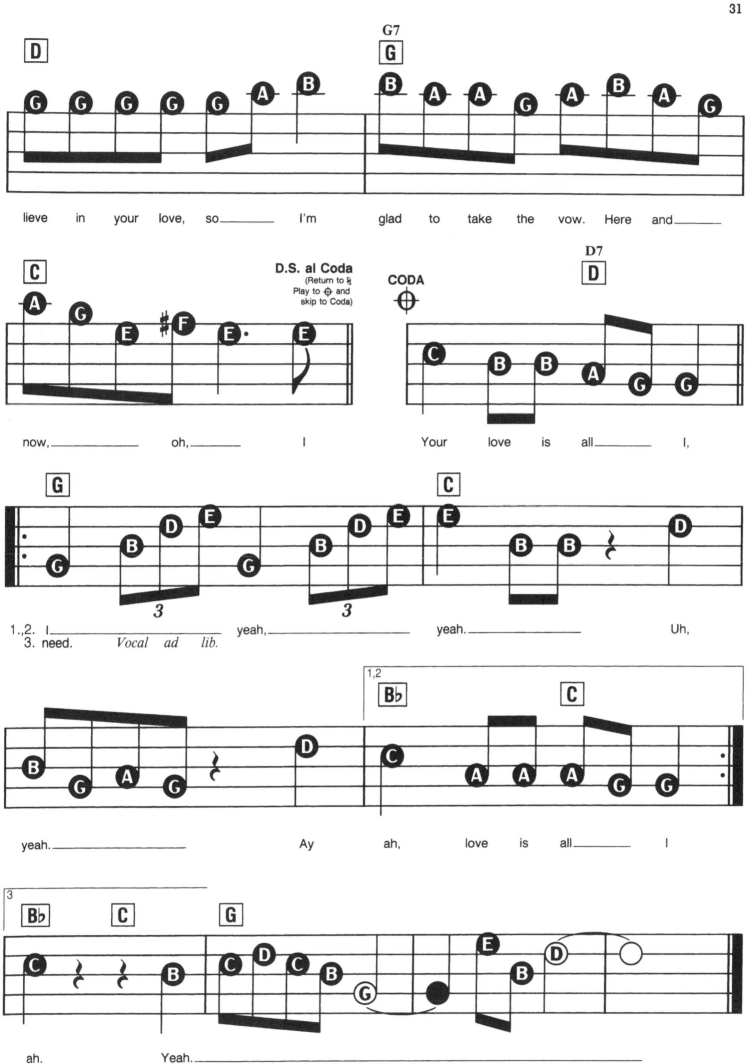

Hello

Registration 1
Rhythm: Slow Rock or Ballad

Words and Music by
Lionel Richie

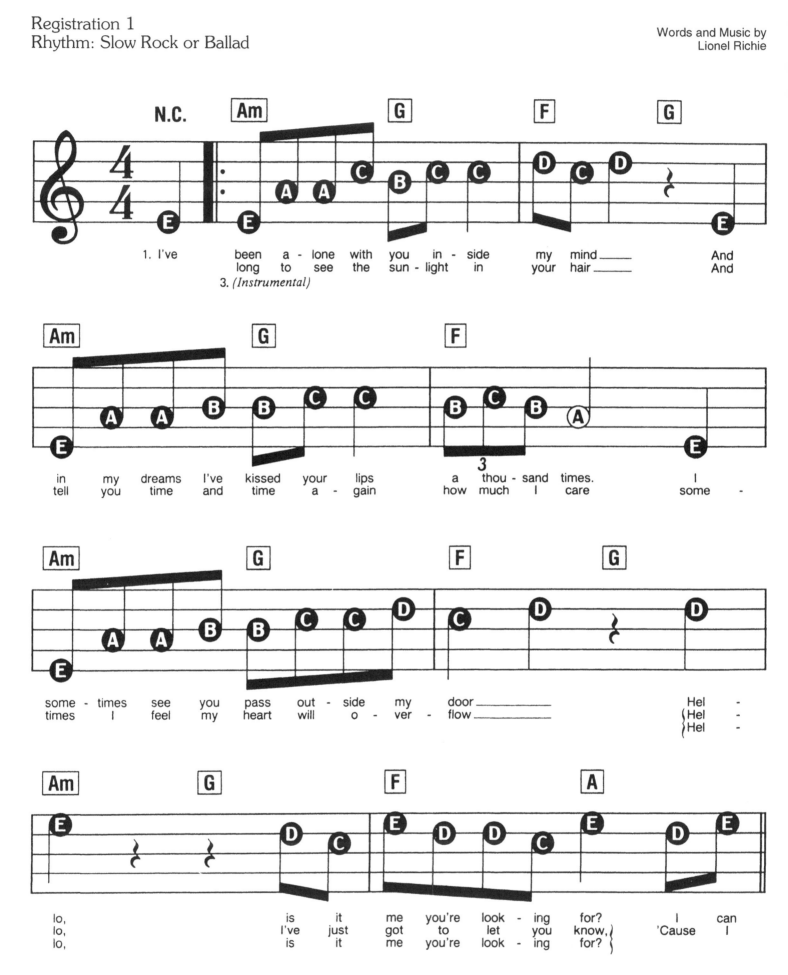

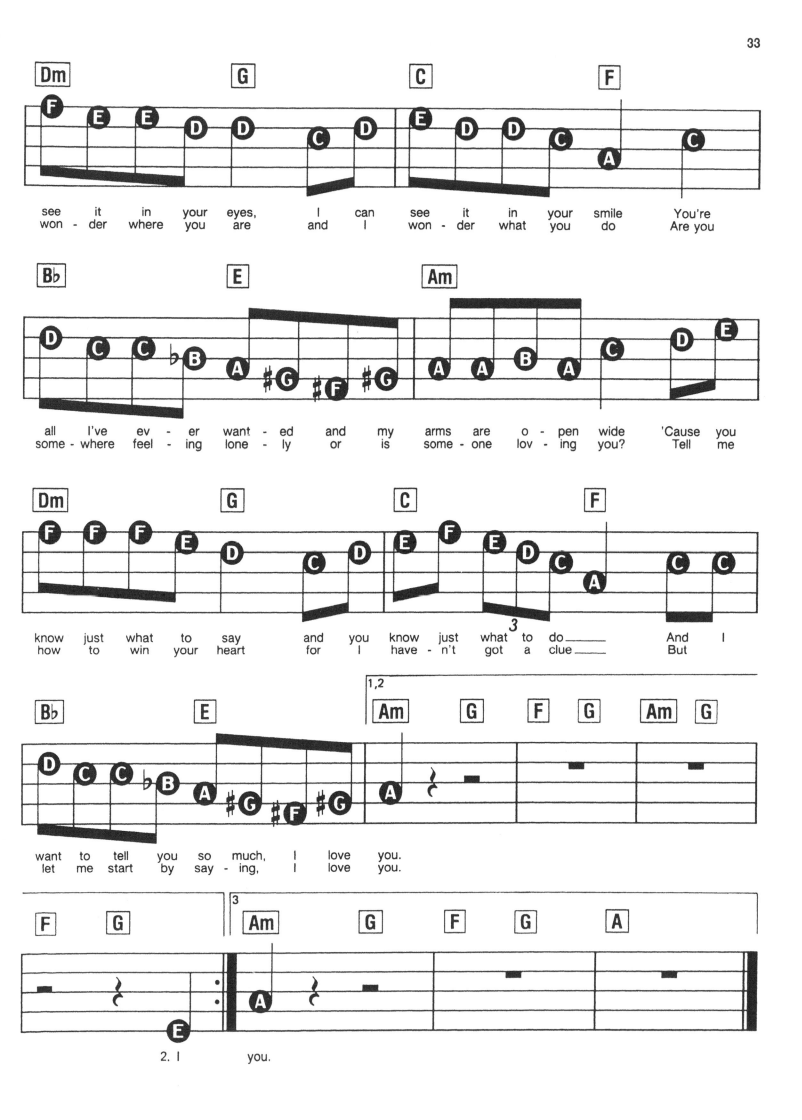

I Honestly Love You

Registration 1
Rhythm: 8 Beat or Pops

Words and Music by Peter Allen
and Jeff Barry

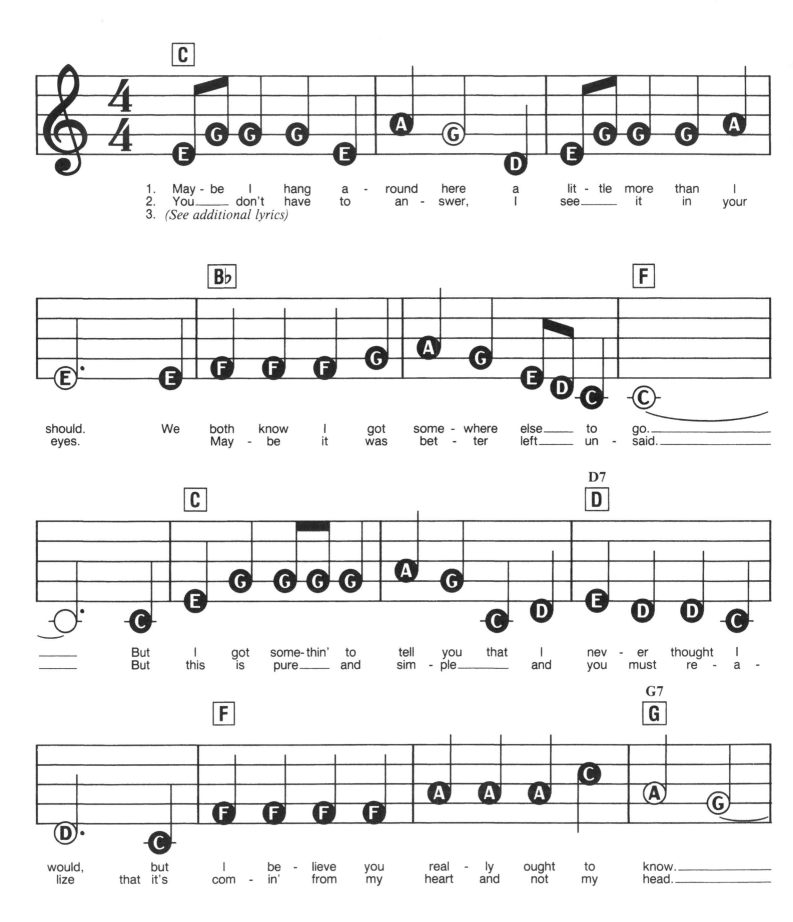

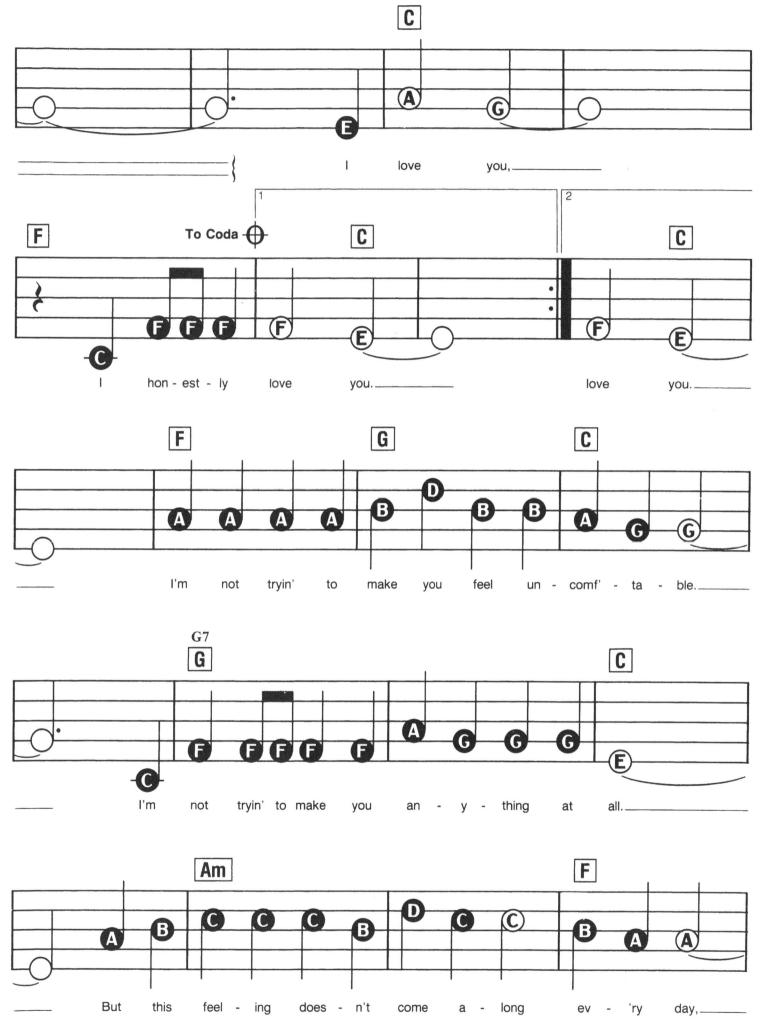

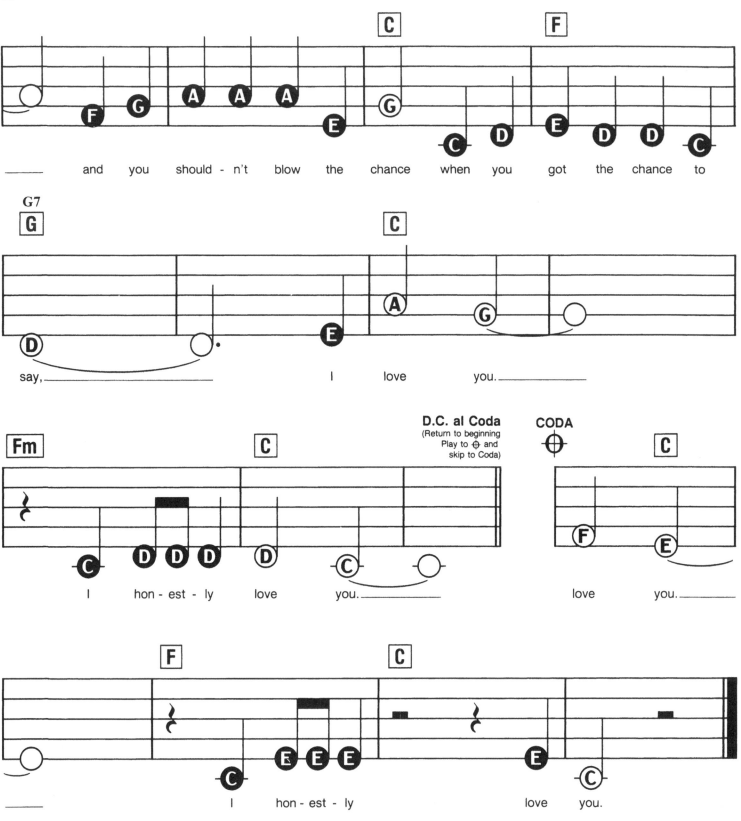

Additional Lyrics

3. If we were both born
   In another place and time,
   This moment might be ending with a kiss,
   But there you are with yours
   And here am I with mine.
   So I guess we'll just be leaving it at this,
   I love you.
   I honestly love you.
   I honestly love you.

Lady in Red

Registration 1
Rhythm: 8 Beat or Pops

Words and Music by
Chris DeBurgh

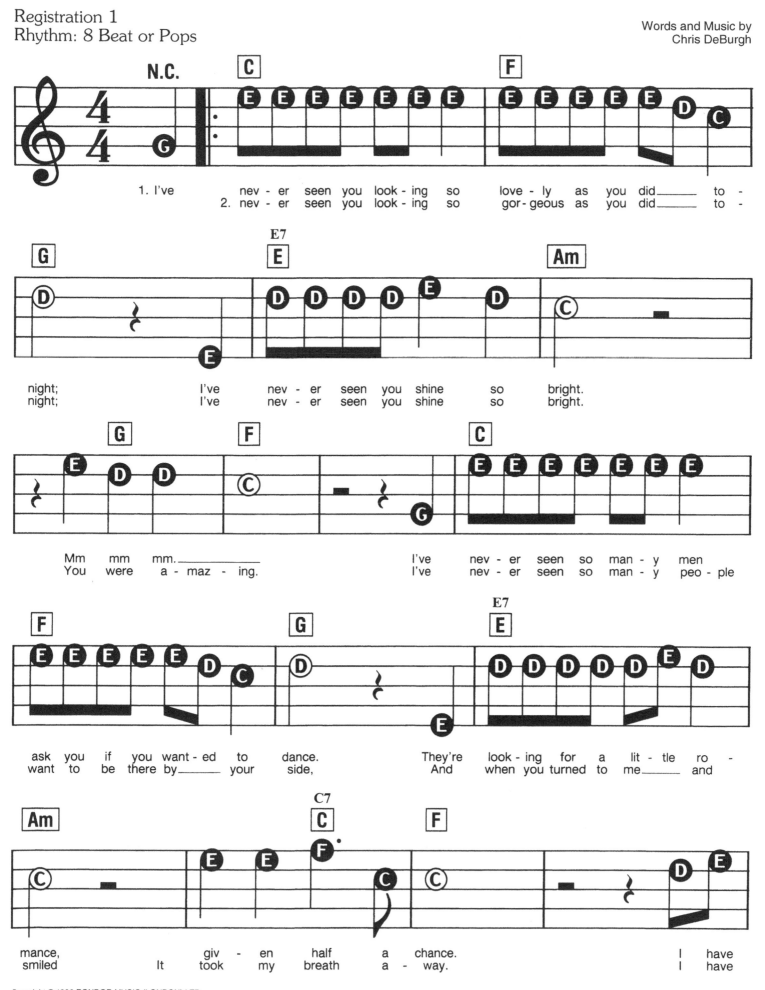

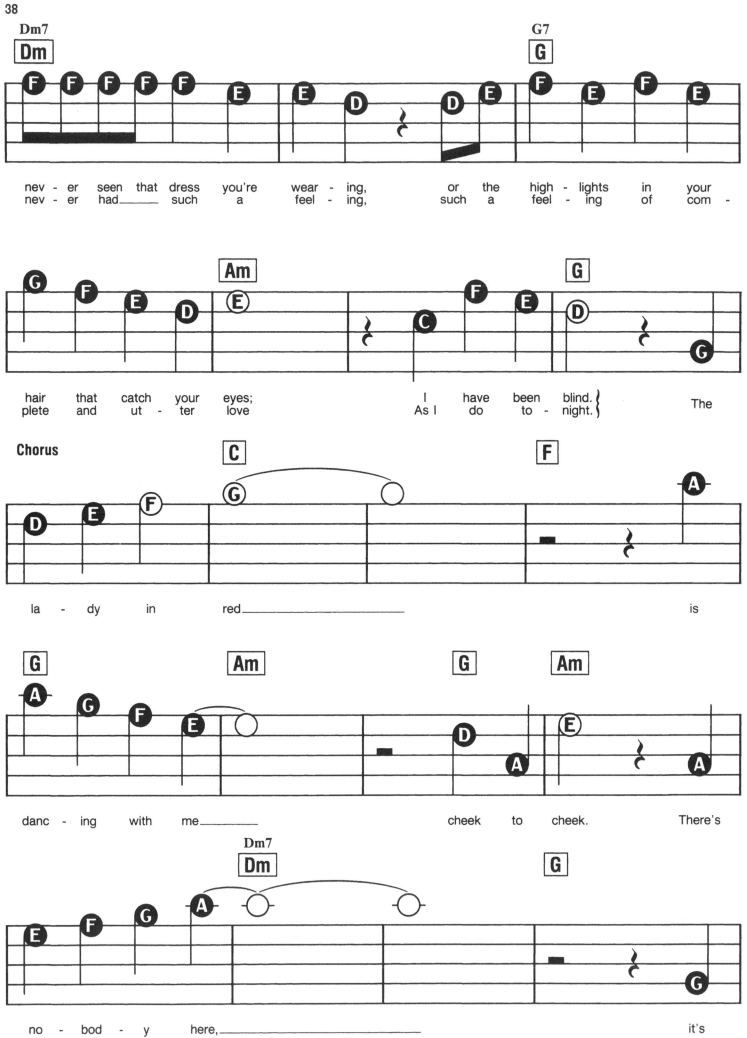

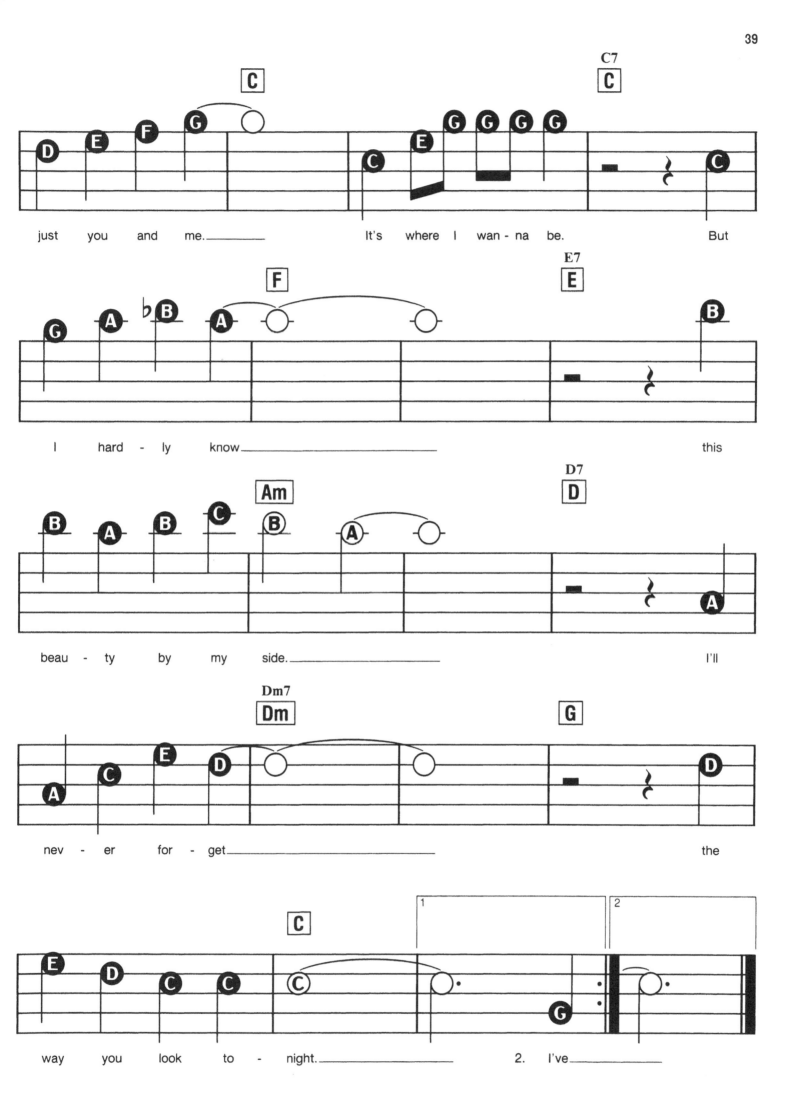

I Just Called to Say I Love You

Registration 2
Rhythm: Rock

Words and Music by
Stevie Wonder

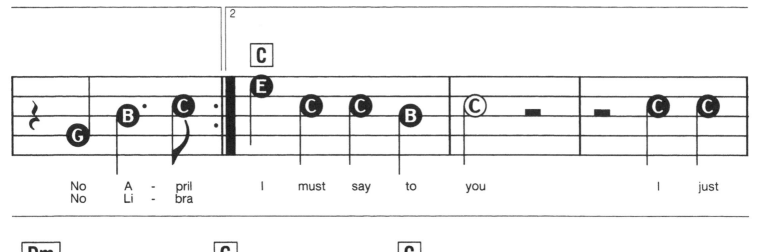

No A - pril
No Li - bra

I must say to you

I just

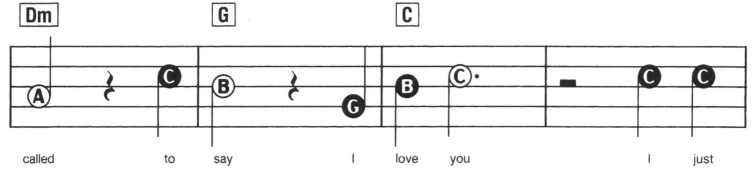

called to say I love you I just

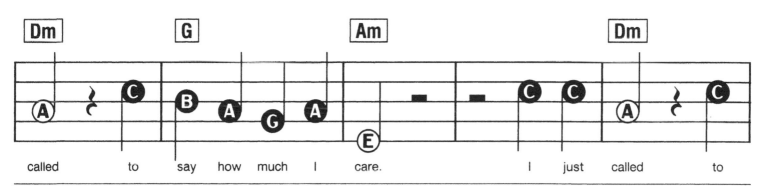

called to say how much I care. I just called to

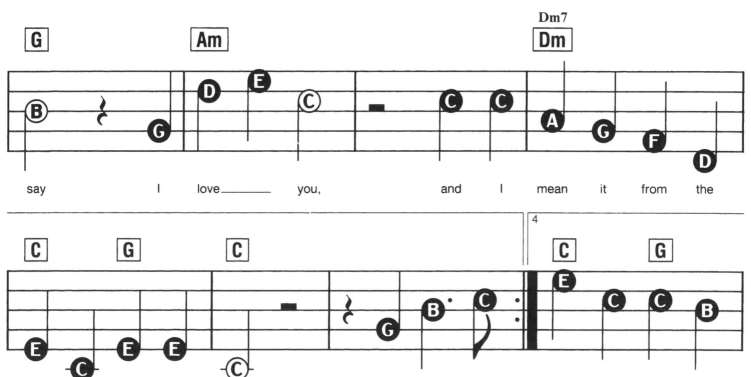

say I love_____ you, and I mean it from the

bot - tom of my heart. No sum - mer's words could ev - er

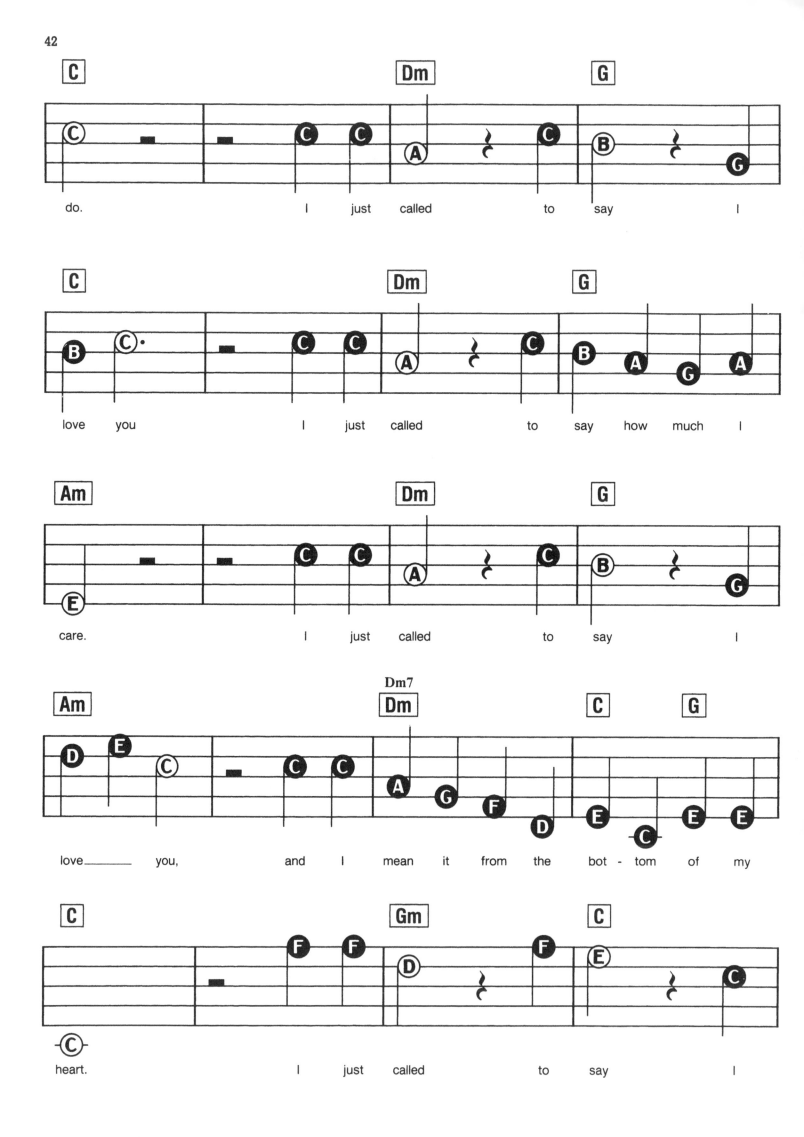

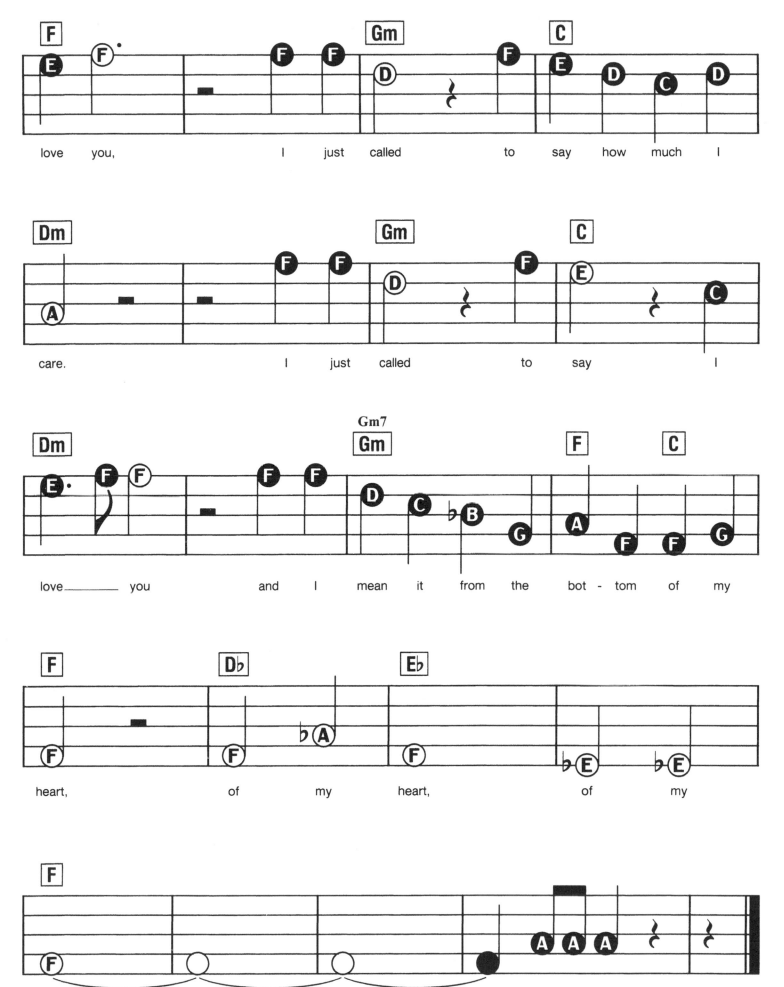

I Will Remember You
Theme from THE BROTHERS McMULLEN

Registration 8
Rhythm: Ballad

Words and Music by Sarah McLachlan,
Seamus Egan and Dave Merenda

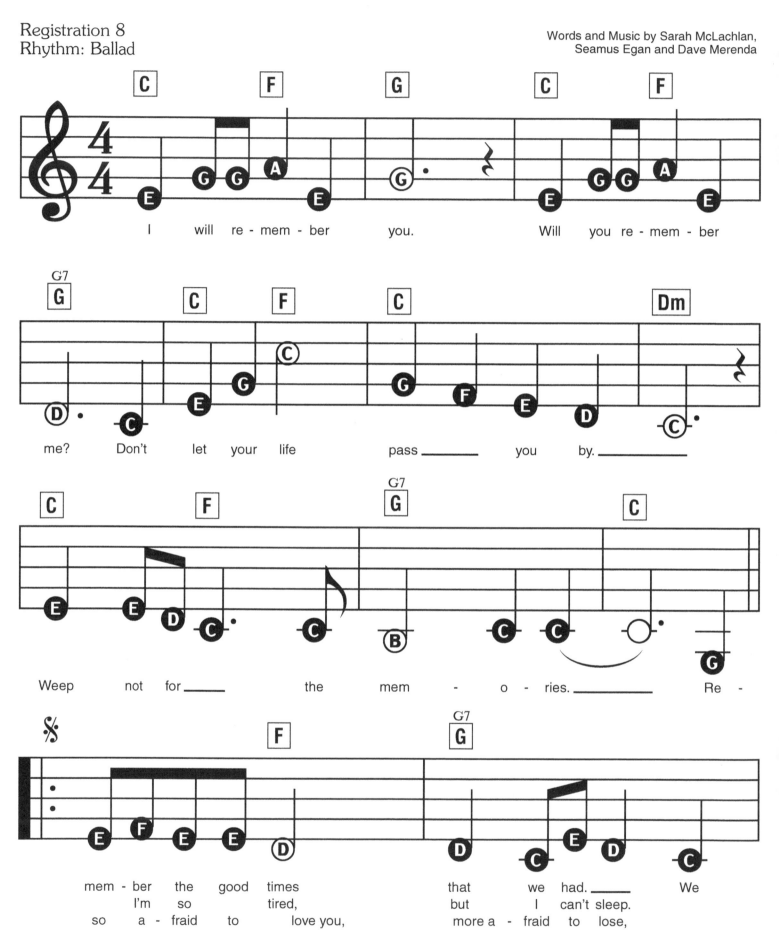

45

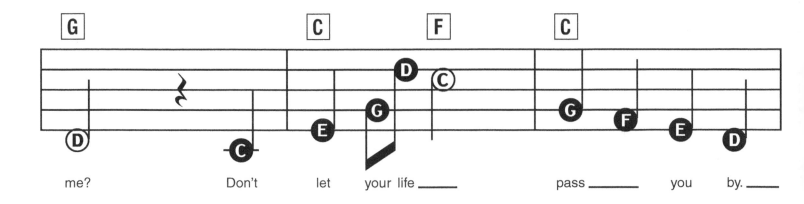

me?   Don't   let   your life ____   pass ____ you   by. ____

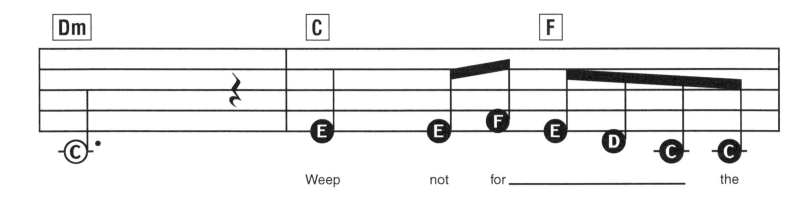

Weep   not   for _____ the

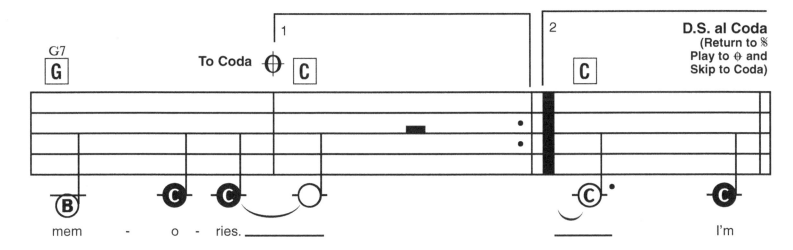

mem - o - ries. _____   _____ I'm

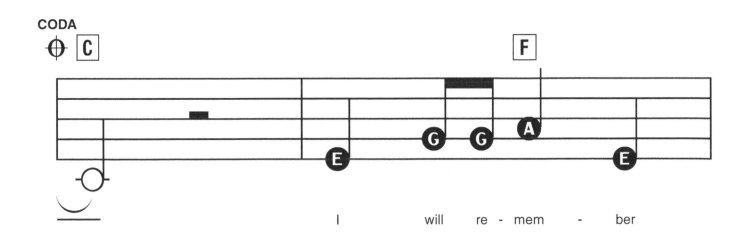

_____   I   will   re - mem - ber

47

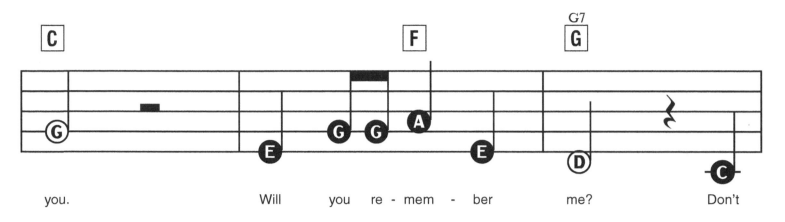

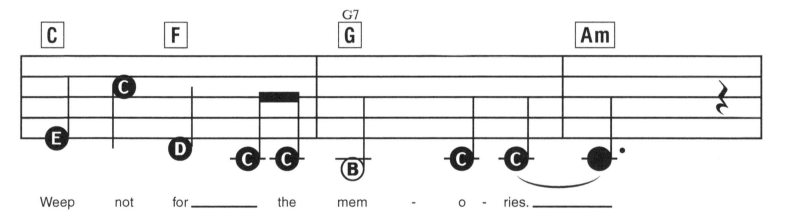

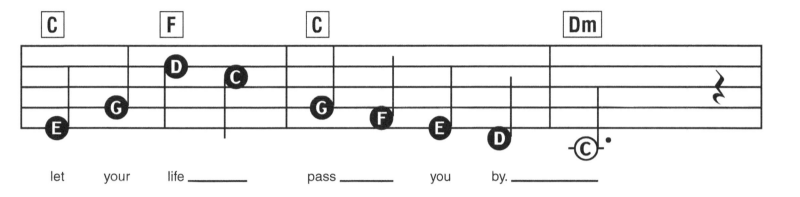

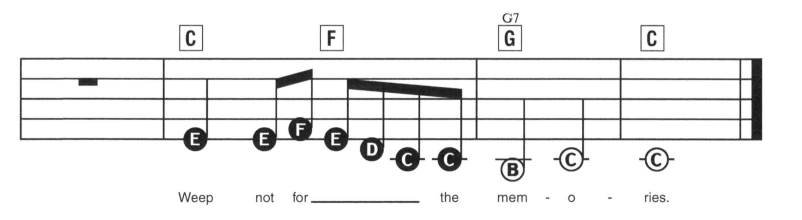

My Cherie Amour

Registration 7
Rhythm: Rock or Bossa Nova

Words and Music by Stevie Wonder,
Sylvia Moy and Henry Cosby

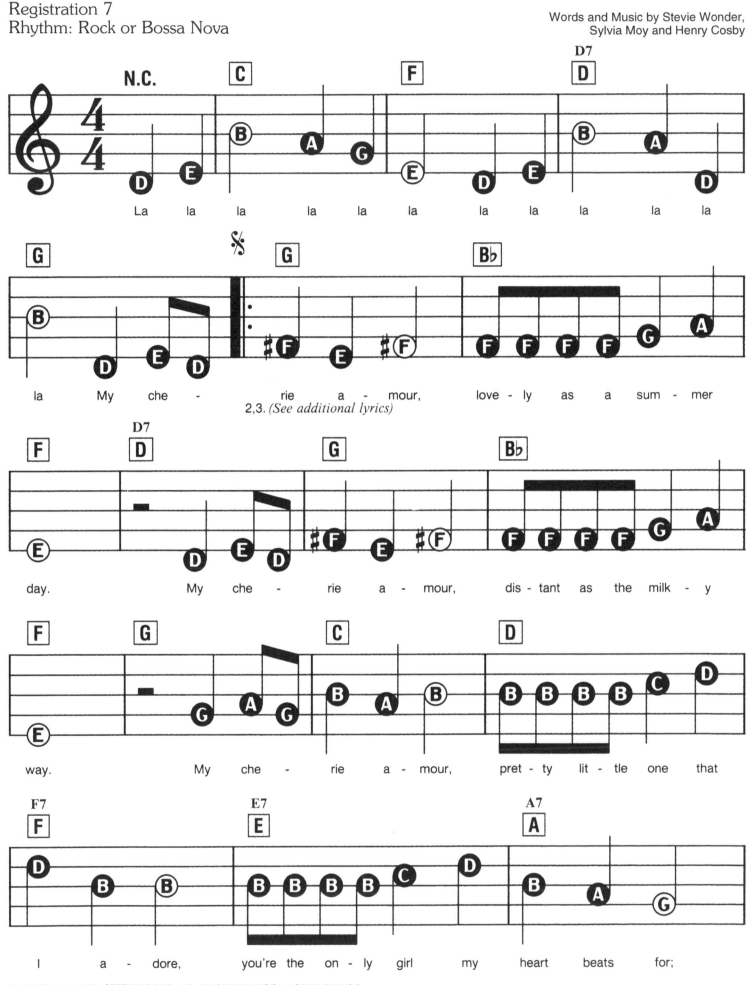

49

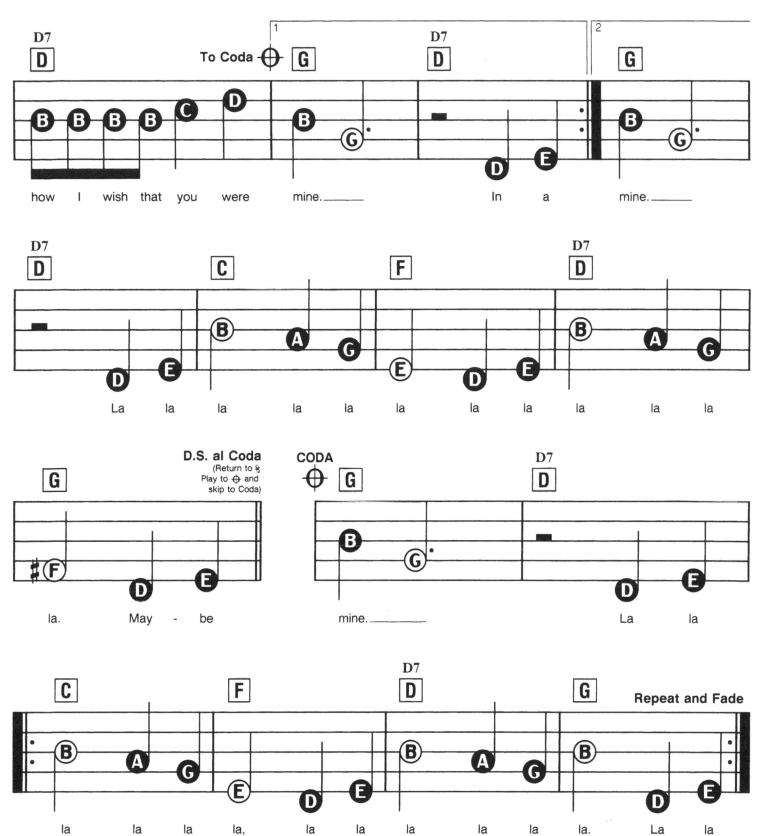

Additional Lyrics

2. In a cafe, or sometimes on a crowded street,
   I've been near you, but you never notice me.
   My cherie amour, won't you tell me how could you ignore,
   That behind that little smile I wore, how I wish that you were mine.

3. Maybe someday you'll see my face among the crowd;
   Maybe someday I'll share your little distant cloud.
   Oh, cherie amour, pretty little one that I adore,
   You're the only girl my heart beats for; how I wish that you were mine.

My Love

Registration 10
Rhythm: Ballad

Words and Music by
Paul and Linda McCartney

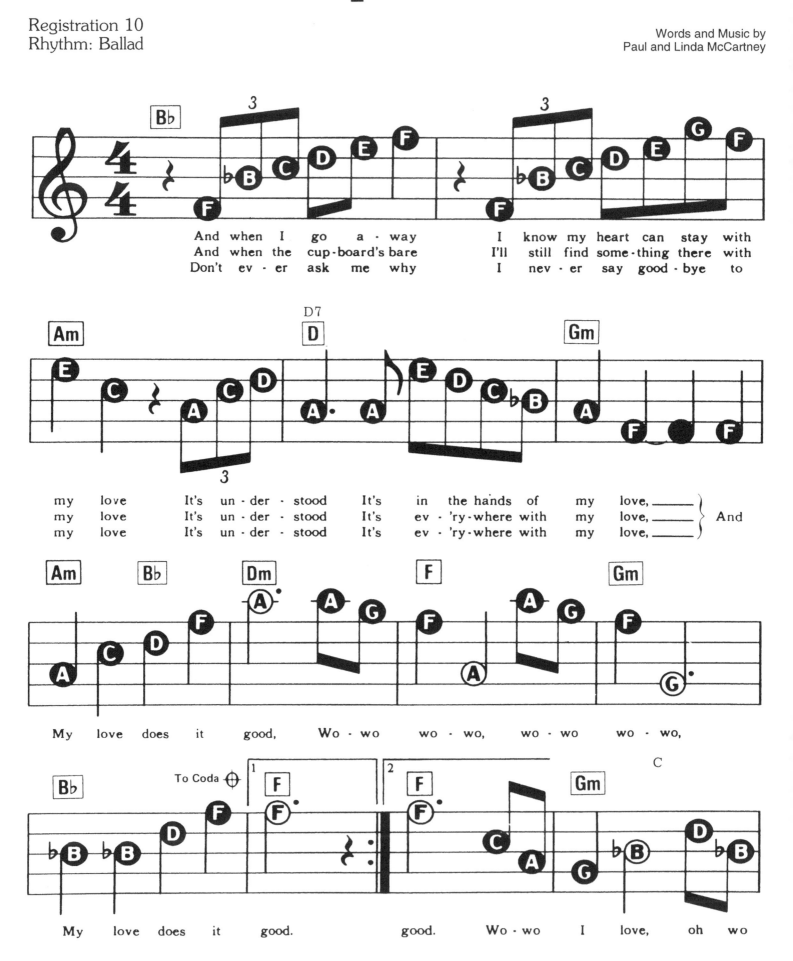

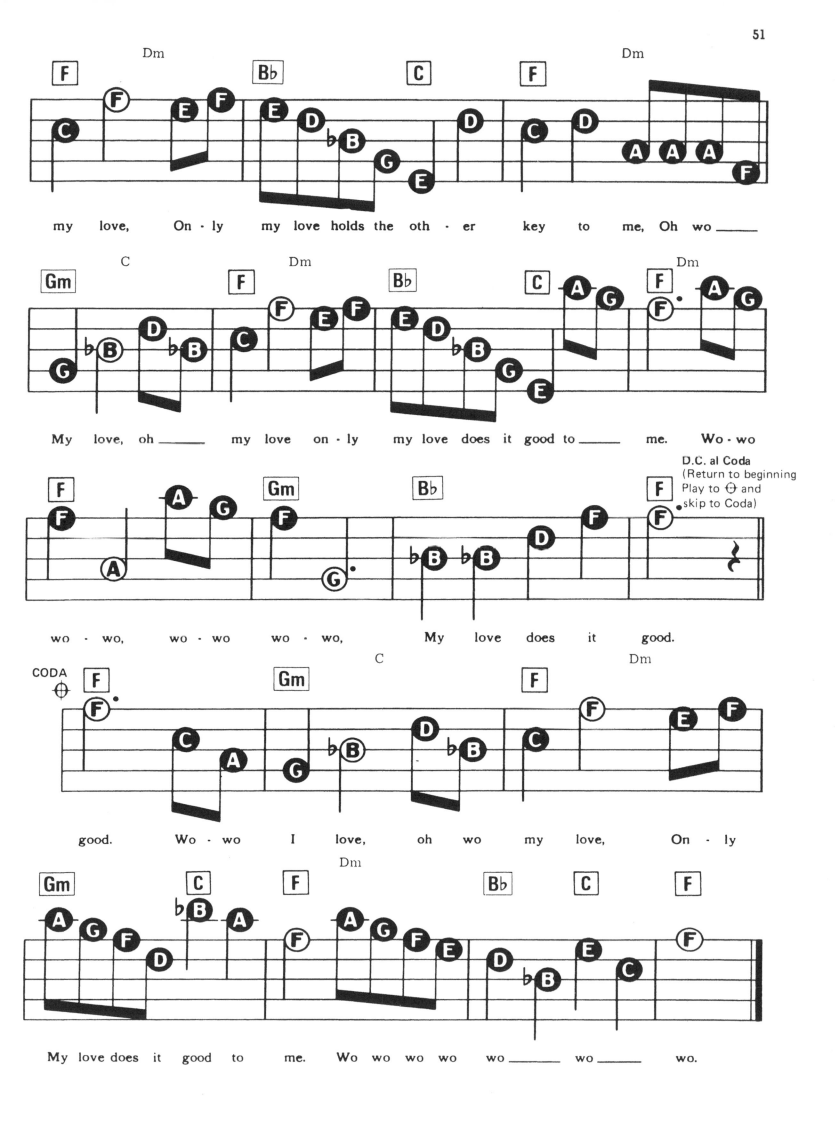

On the Wings of Love

Registration 3
Rhythm: 8 Beat or Pops

Words and Music by Jeffrey Osborne
and Peter Schless

1. Just smile for me and let___ the day___ be - gin.
2. *(See additional lyrics)*

You are the sun - shine that lights my heart___ with - in.

And I'm sure that you're___ an an - gel in___ dis - guise.

Come take my hand and to - geth - er we___ will ride.

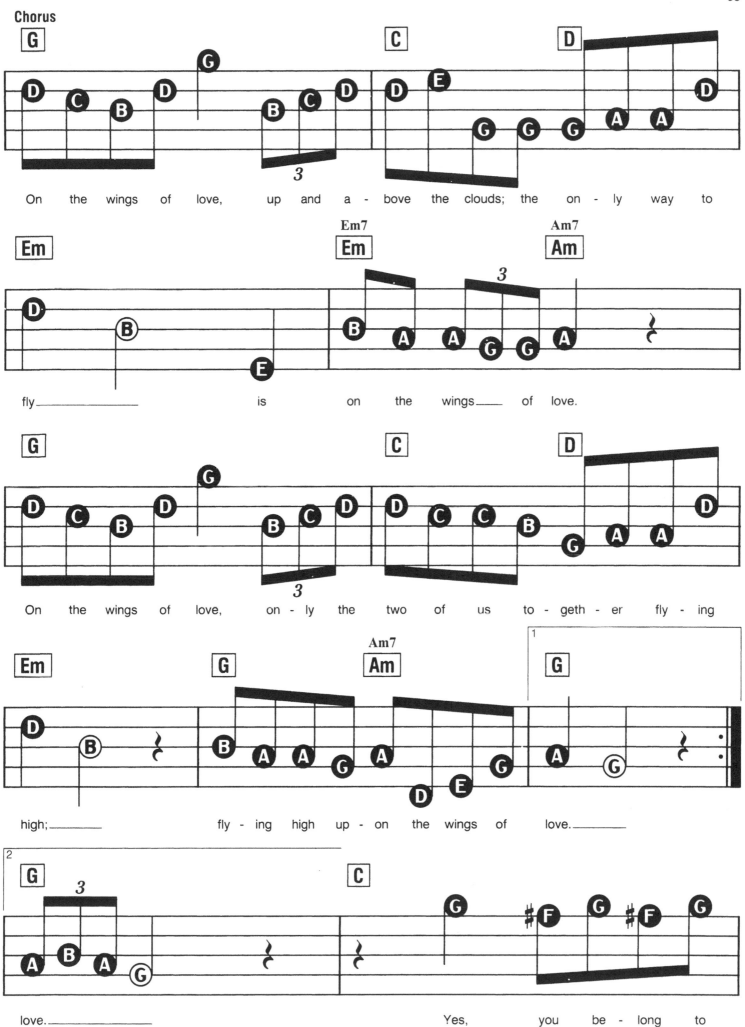

54

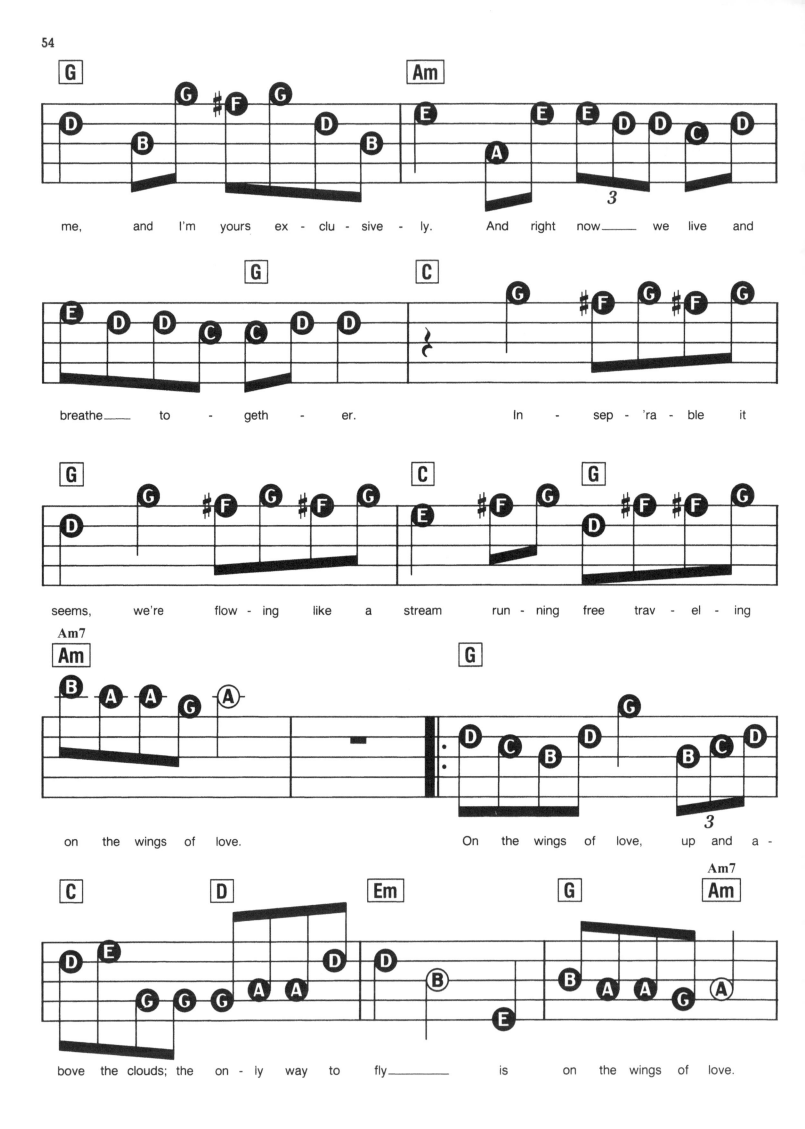

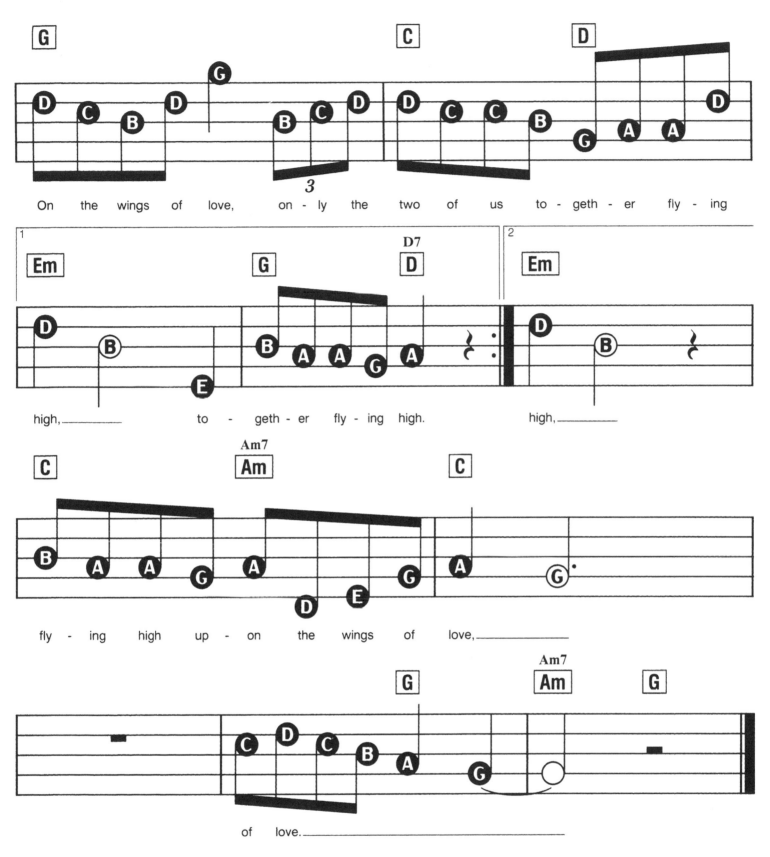

On the wings of love, on - ly the two of us to - geth - er fly - ing

high,_____ to - geth - er fly - ing high. high,_____

fly - ing high up - on the wings of love,_____

of love._____

Additional Lyrics

2. You look at me and I begin to melt
   Just like the snow, when a ray of sun is felt.
   And I'm crazy 'bout you, baby, can't you see?
   I'd be so delighted if you would come with me.

   (To Chorus:)

She's Got a Way

Registration 3
Rhythm: Ballad

Words and Music by
Billy Joel

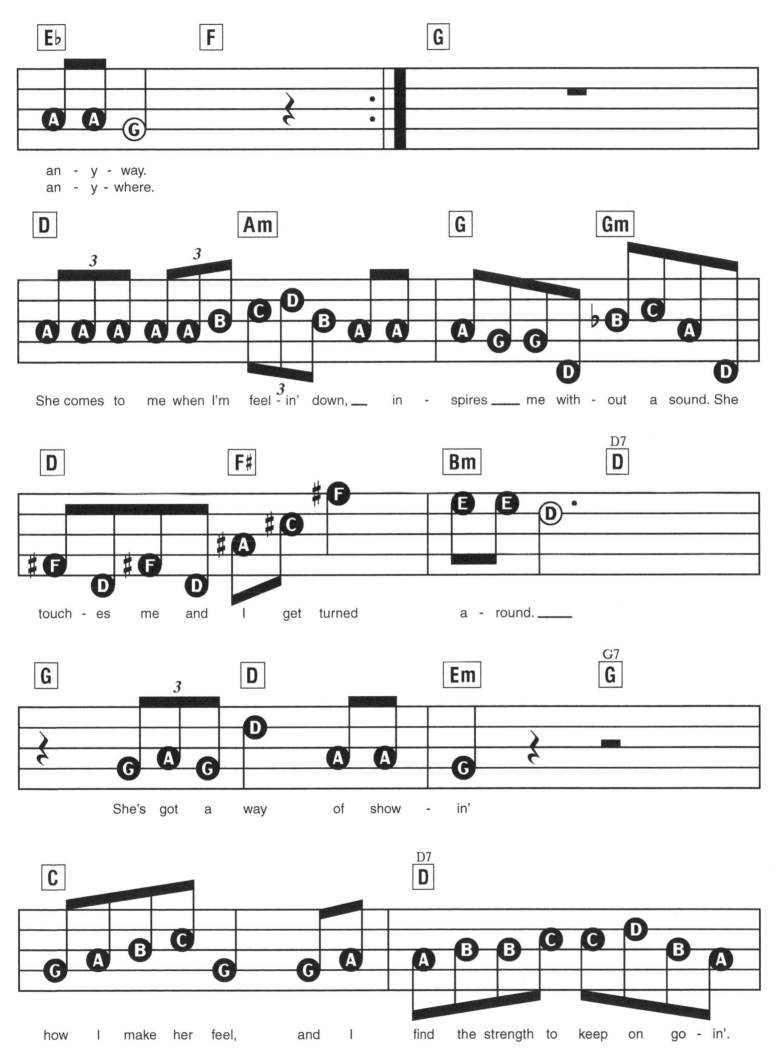

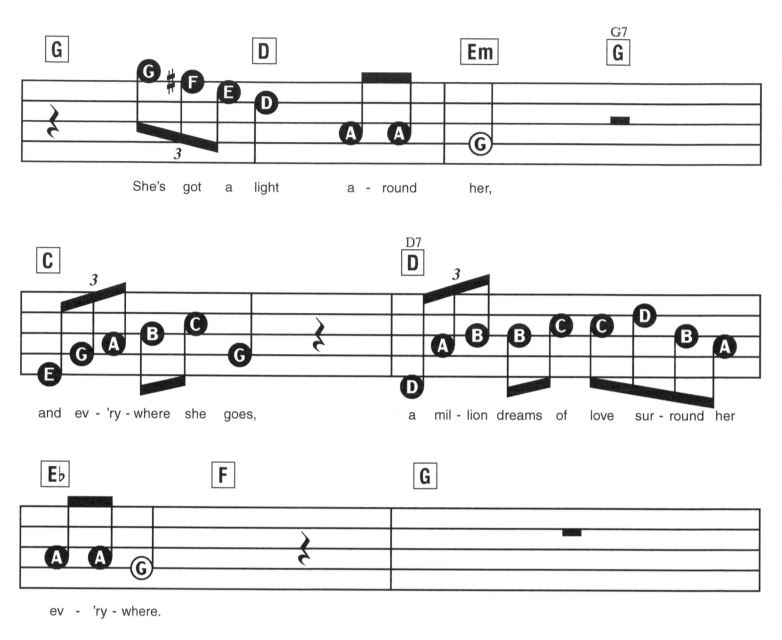

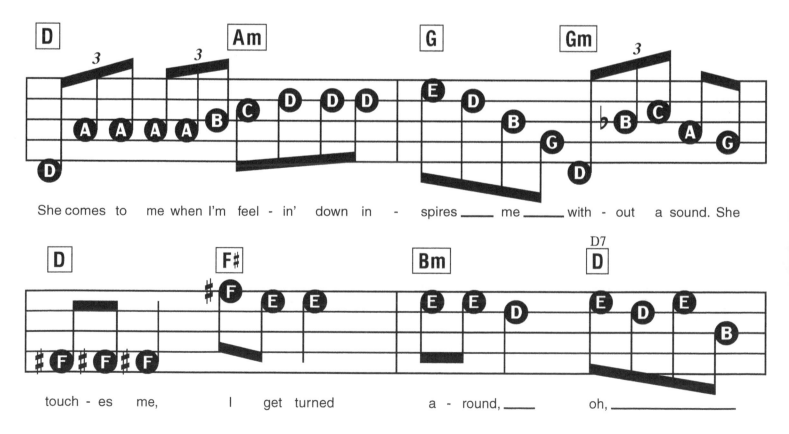

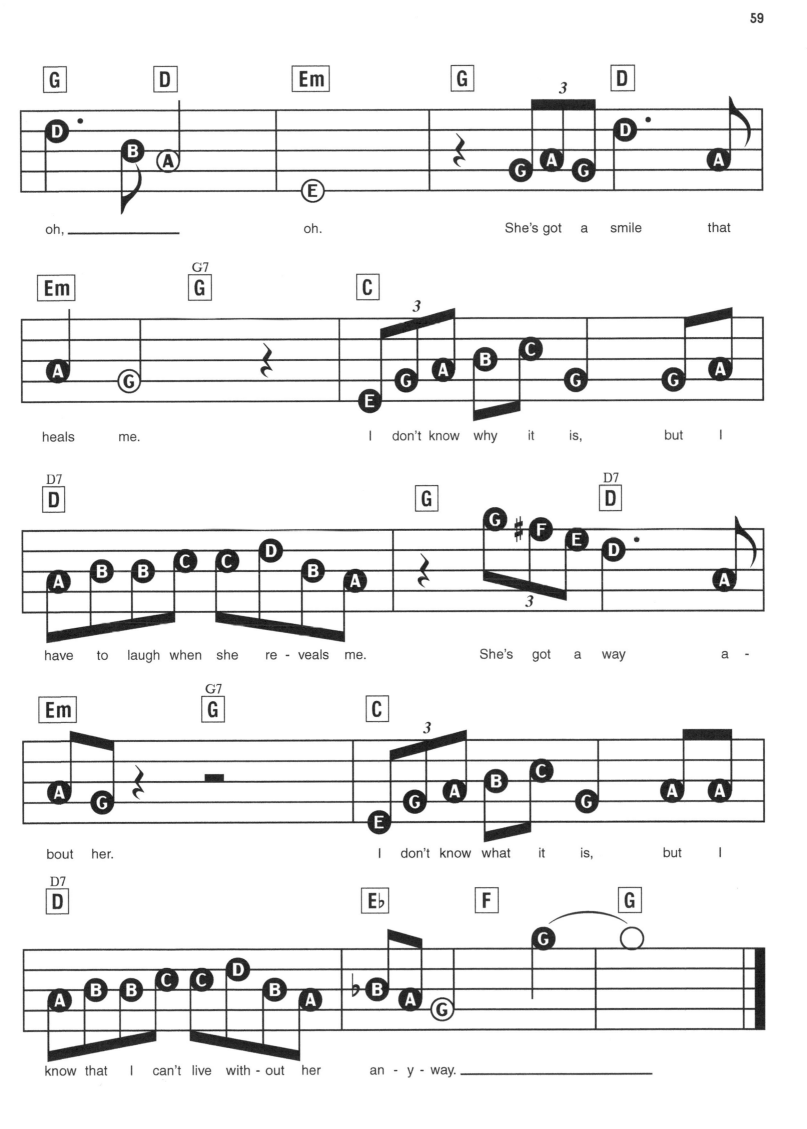

Sweet Love

Registration 5
Rhythm: 8 Beat or Pops

Words and Music by Gary Bias,
Louis A. Johnson and Anita Baker

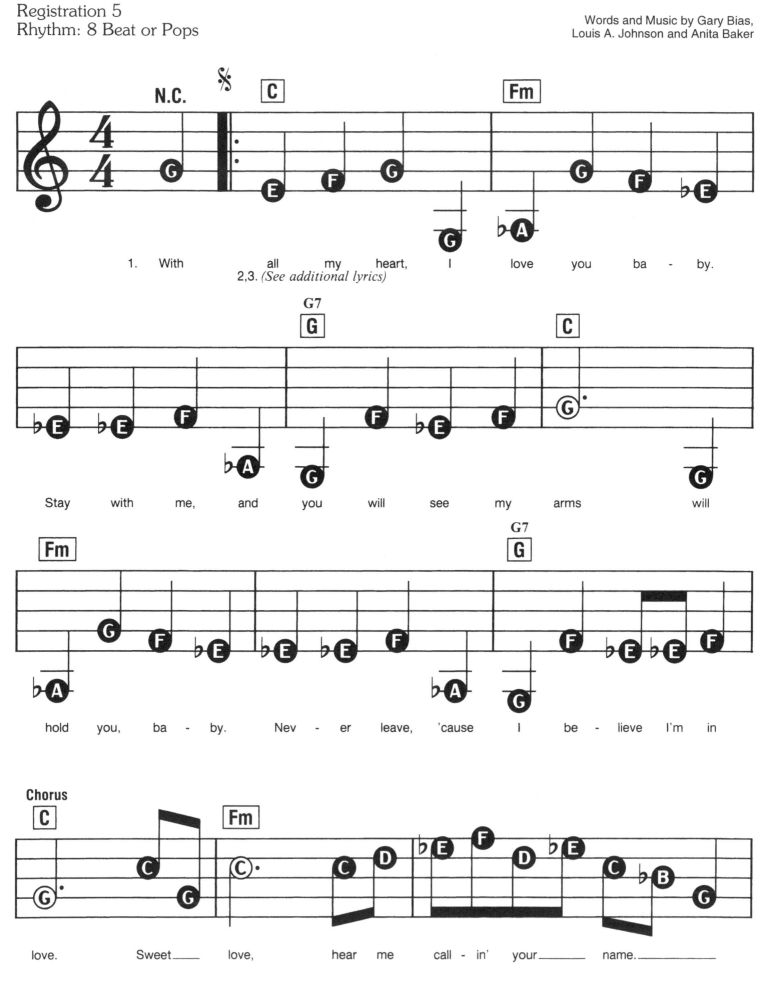

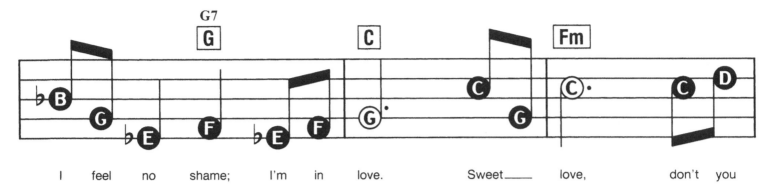

I feel no shame; I'm in love. Sweet___ love, don't you

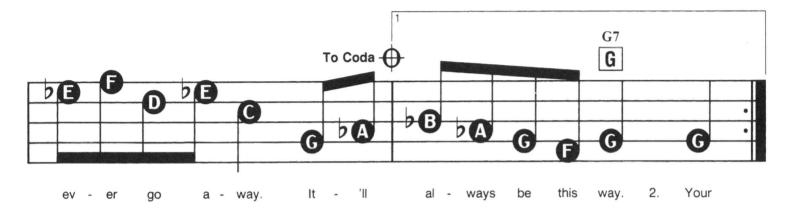

ev - er go a - way. It - 'll al - ways be this way. 2. Your

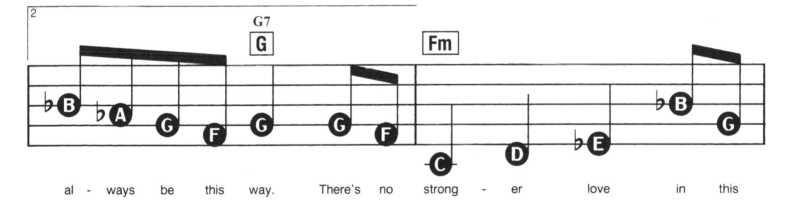

al - ways be this way. There's no strong - er love in this

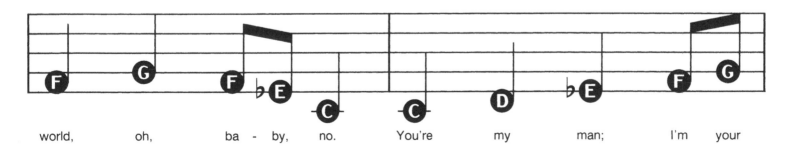

world, oh, ba - by, no. You're my man; I'm your

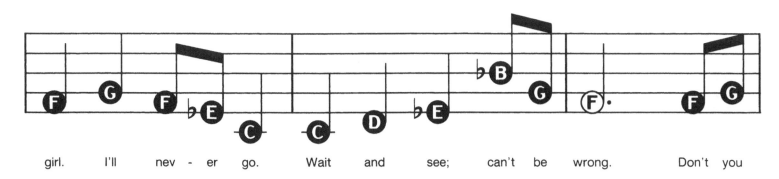

girl.   I'll   nev - er   go.   Wait   and   see;   can't   be   wrong.   Don't you

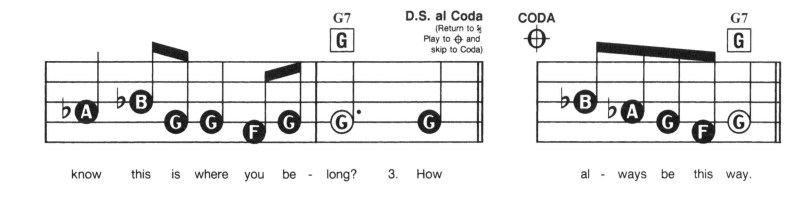

D.S. al Coda
(Return to %
Play to ⊕ and
skip to Coda)

CODA

know   this   is   where   you   be - long?   3. How   al - ways   be   this   way.

Repeat and Fade

Sweet   love.

Additional Lyrics

2. Your heart has called me closer to you.
I will be all that you need.
Just trust in what we're feeling.
Never leave, 'cause baby, I believe
In this love.

(To Chorus:)

3. How sweet this dream, how lovely, baby.
Stay right here, never fear.
I will be all that you need.
Never leave, 'cause baby, I believe
In this love.

(To Chorus:)

Up Where We Belong

from the Paramount Picture AN OFFICER AND A GENTLEMAN

Registration 3
Rhythm: Rock

Words by Will Jennings
Music by Buffy Sainte-Marie and Jack Nitzsche

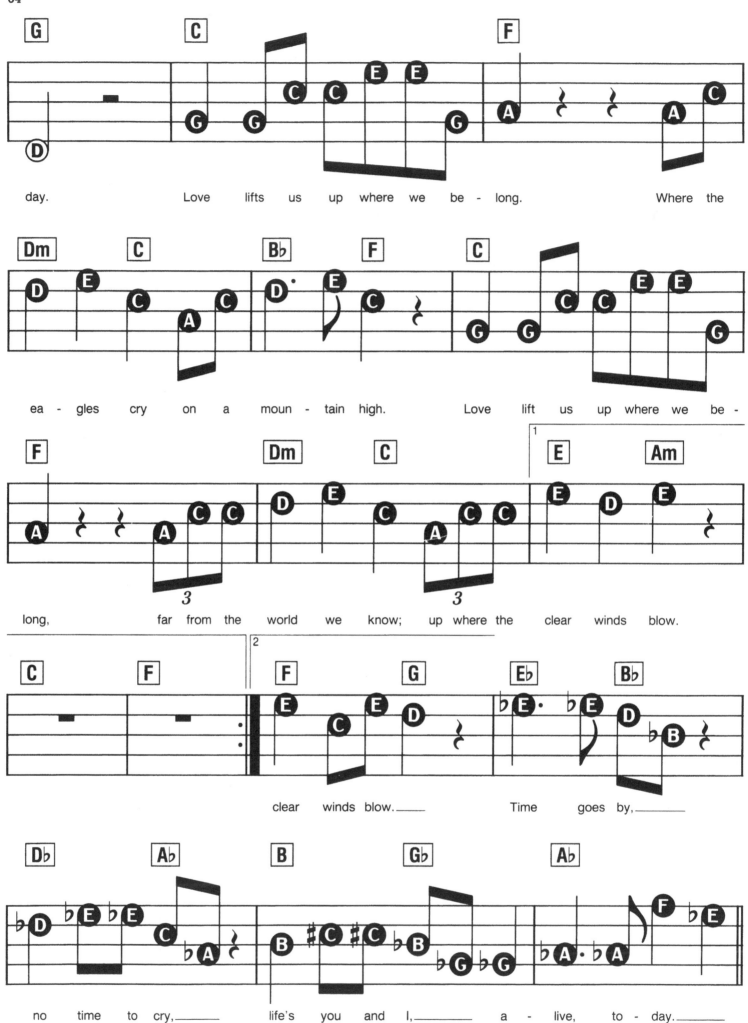

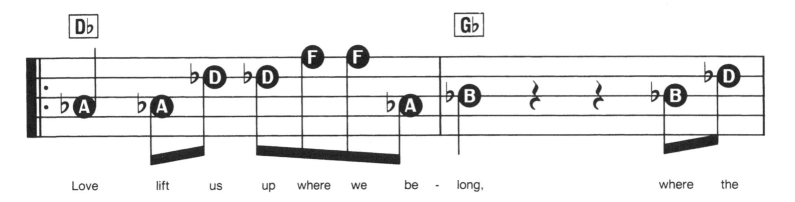

Love   lift   us   up   where   we   be - long,   where   the

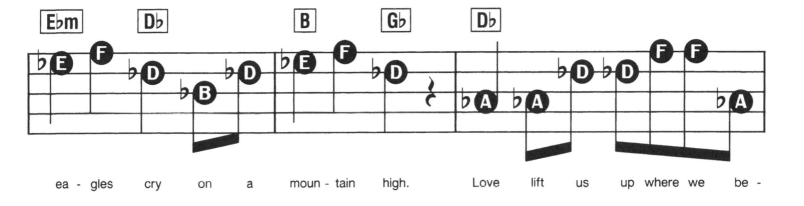

ea - gles   cry   on   a   moun - tain   high.   Love   lift   us   up   where   we   be -

Repeat and Fade

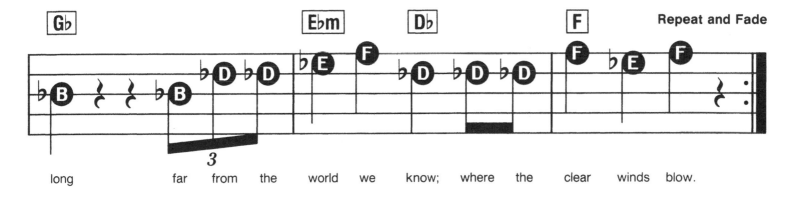

long   far   from   the   world   we   know;   where   the   clear   winds   blow.

2. Some hang on to "used to be,"
   Live their lives looking behind.
   All we have is here and now;
   All our life, out there to find.
   The road is long.
   There are mountains in our way,
   But we climb them a step every day.

Tonight, I Celebrate My Love

Registration 3
Rhythm: Rock or Pops

Music by Michael Masser
Lyric by Gerry Goffin

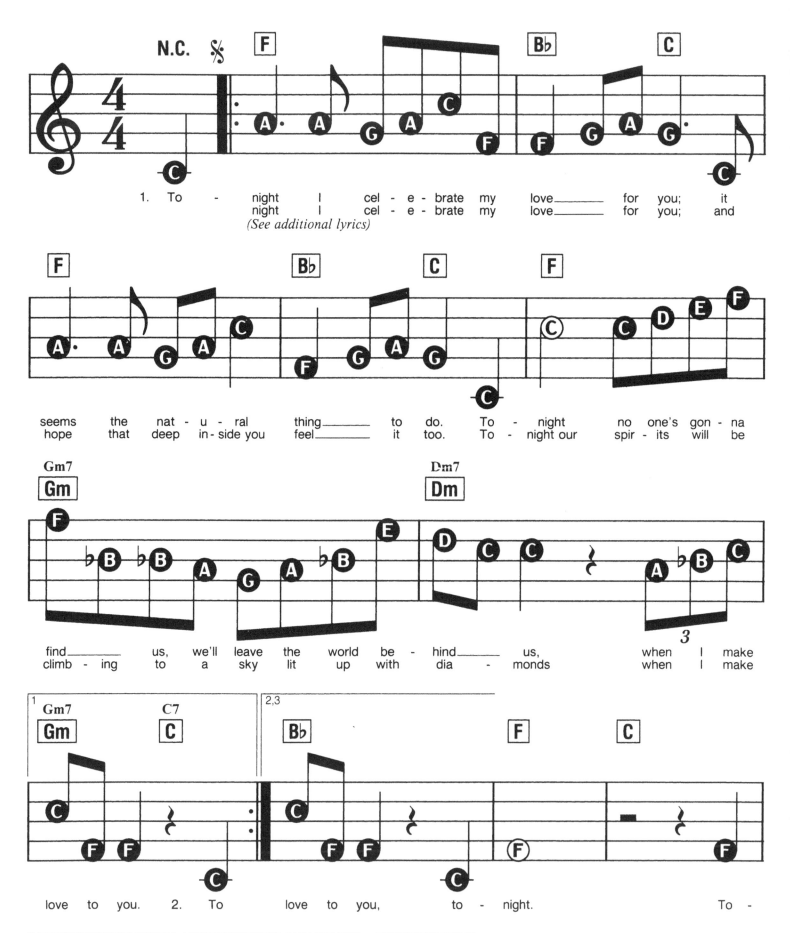

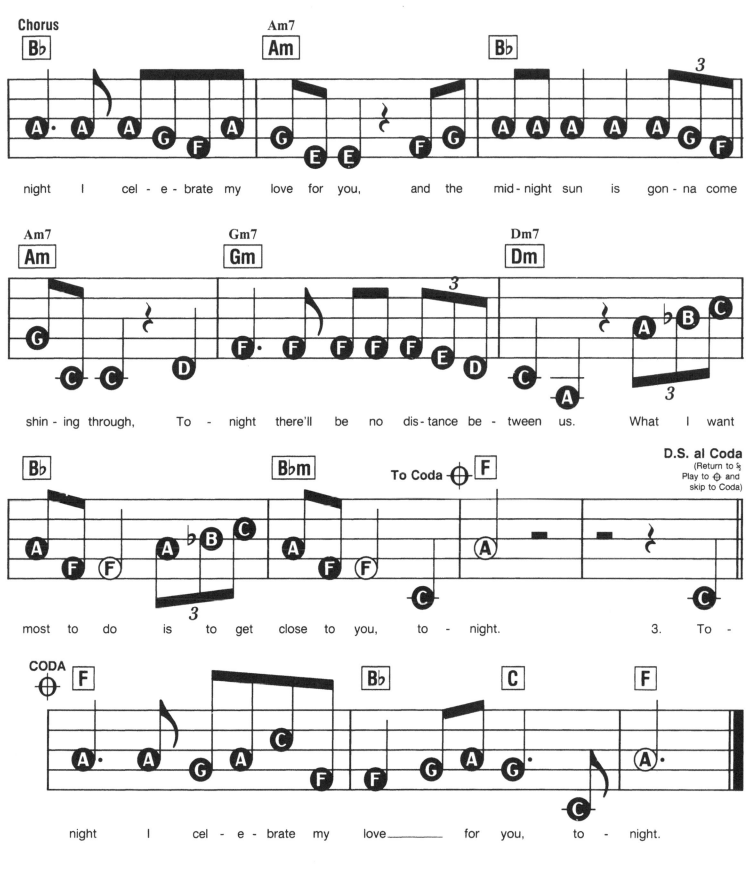

Additional Lyrics

3. Tonight I celebrate my love for you.
And soon this old world will seem brand new.
Tonight we will both discover
How friends turn into lovers,
When I make love to you.
Chorus

We've Only Just Begun

Registration 1
Rhythm: 8 Beat or Pops

Words and Music by Roger Nichols
and Paul Williams

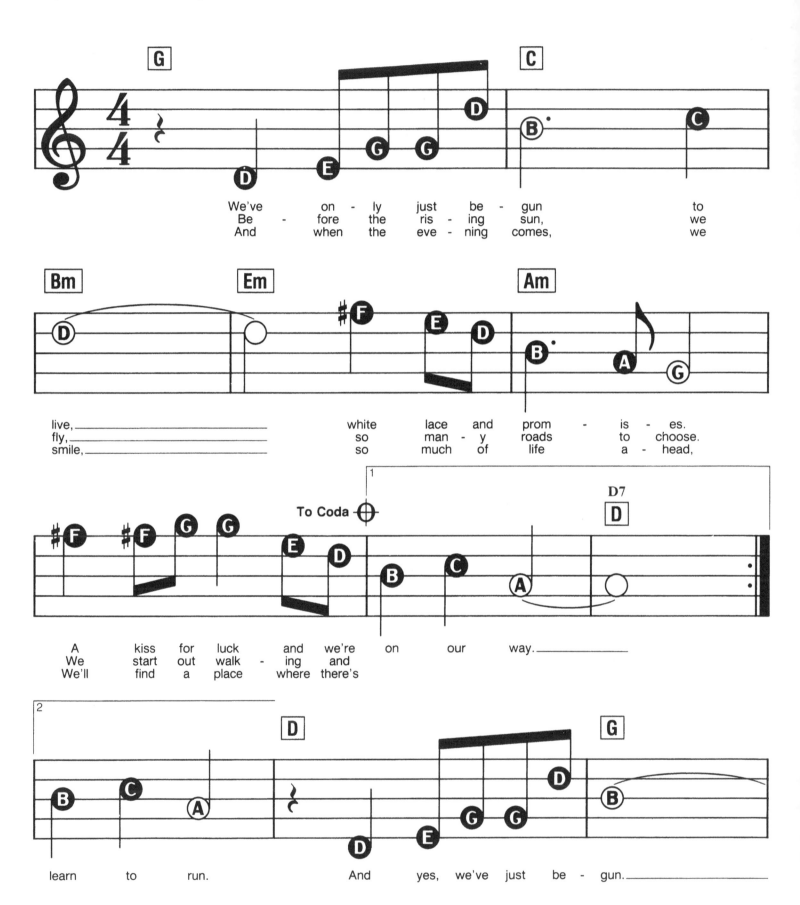

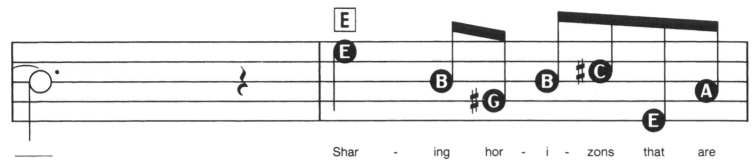

Shar - ing hor - i - zons that are

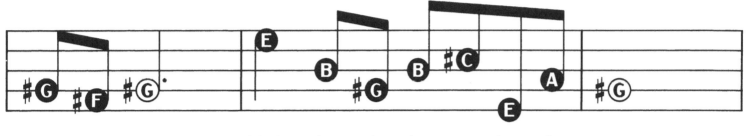

new to us. Watch - ing the signs a - long the way.

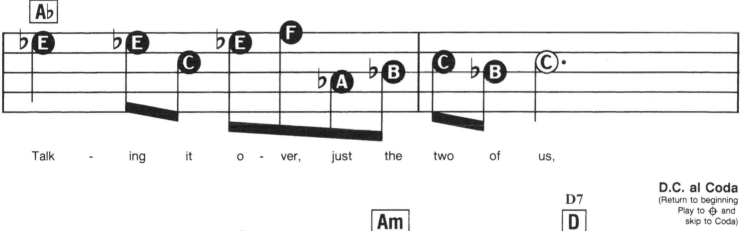

Talk - ing it o - ver, just the two of us,

D.C. al Coda
(Return to beginning
Play to ⊕ and
skip to Coda)

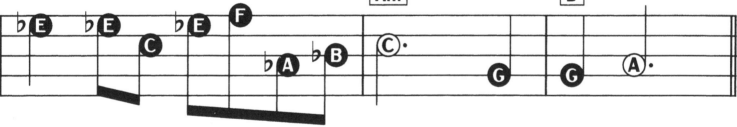

work - ing to - geth - er day to day, to - geth - er.

CODA

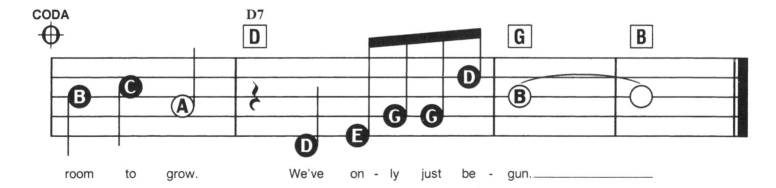

room to grow. We've on - ly just be - gun.

Where Do I Begin
(Love Theme)
from the Paramount Picture LOVE STORY

Registration 8
Rhythm: Ballad or Slow Rock

Words by Carl Sigman
Music by Francis Lai

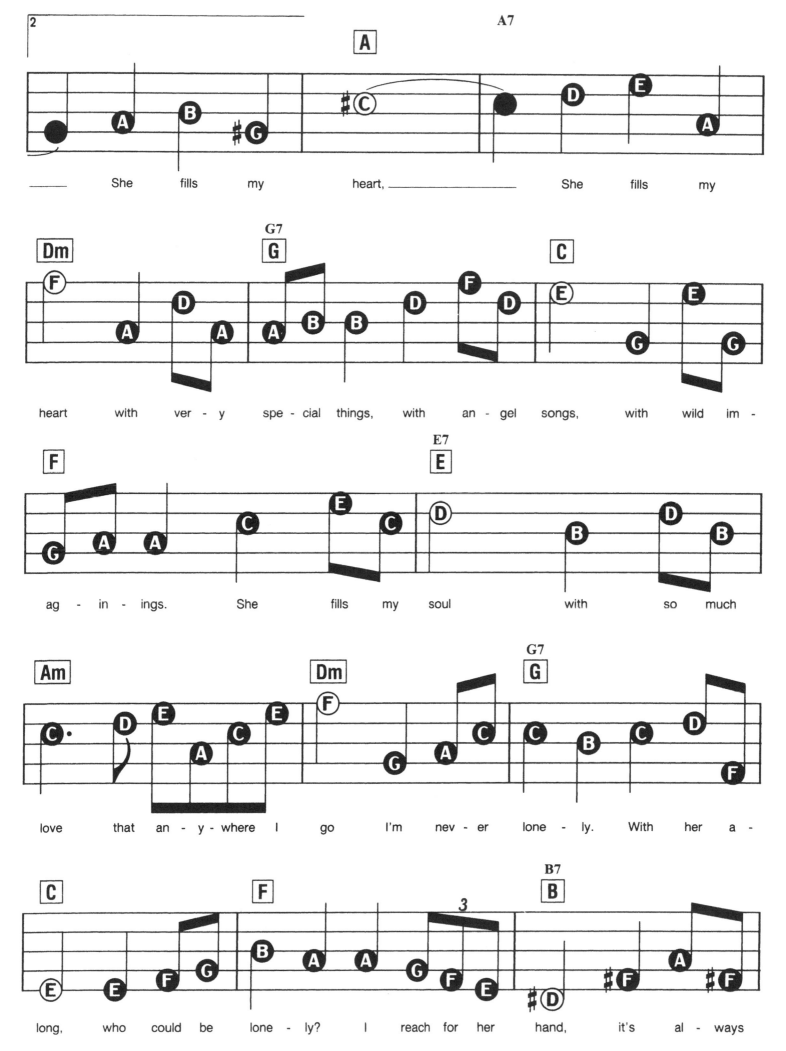

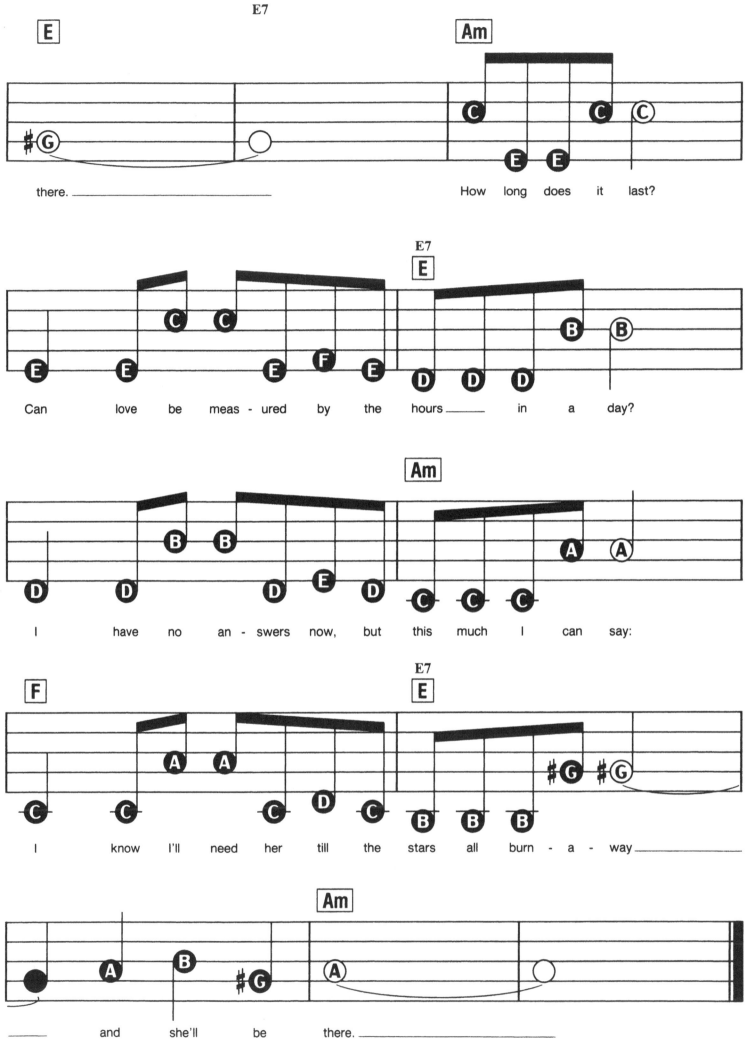

You Light Up My Life

Registration 3
Rhythm: Waltz

Words and Music by
Joseph Brooks

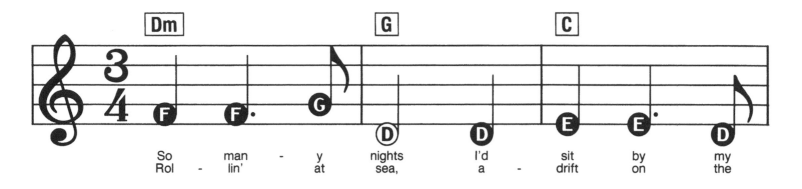

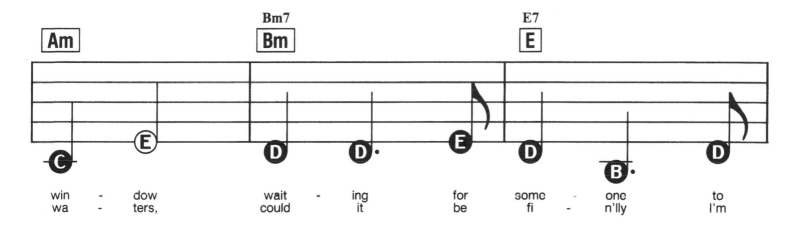

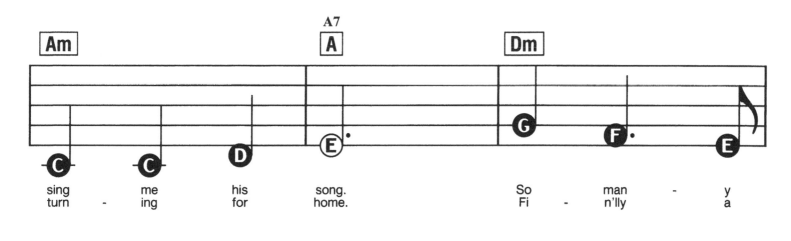

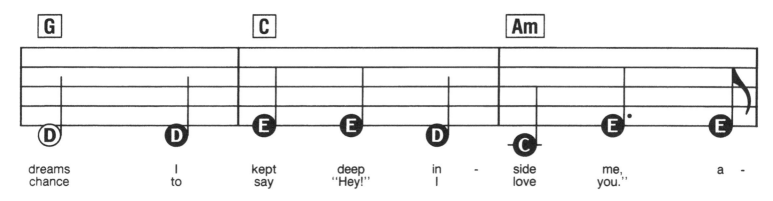

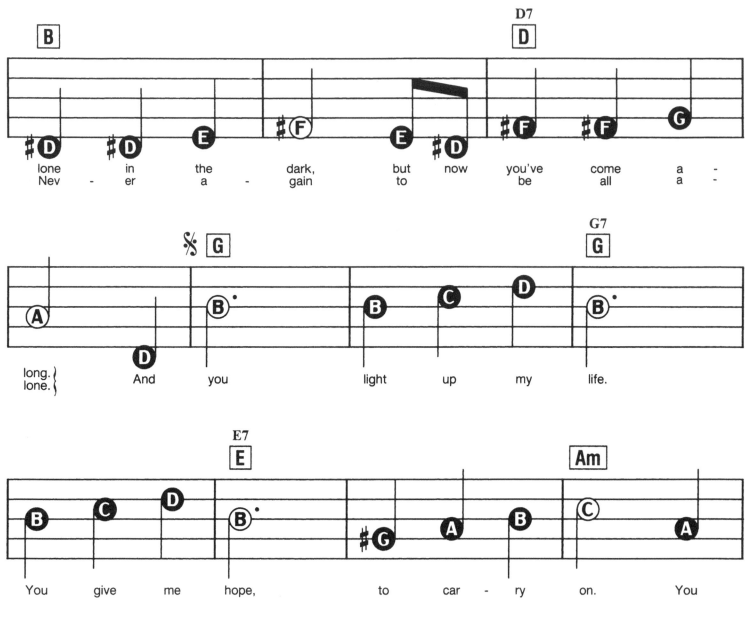

lone - in the dark, but now you've come a -
Nev - er a - gain to be all a -

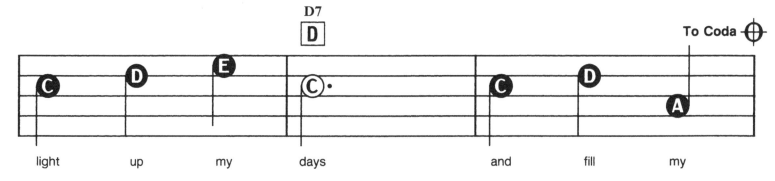

long.
lone. And you light up my life.

You give me hope, to car - ry on. You

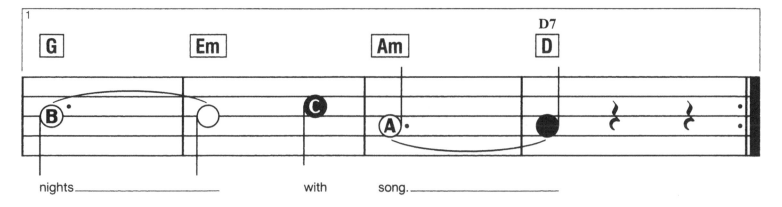

light up my days and fill my

nights_____ with song._____

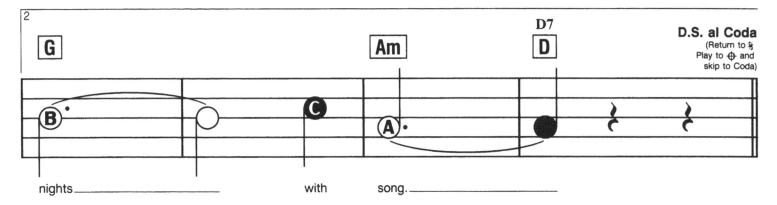

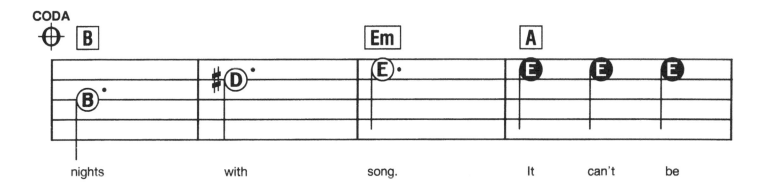

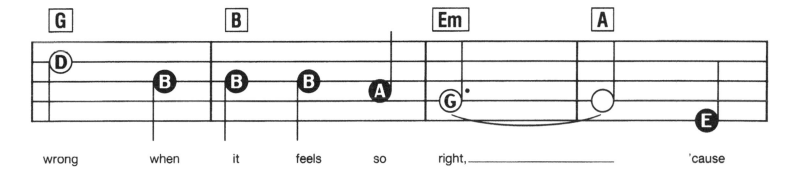

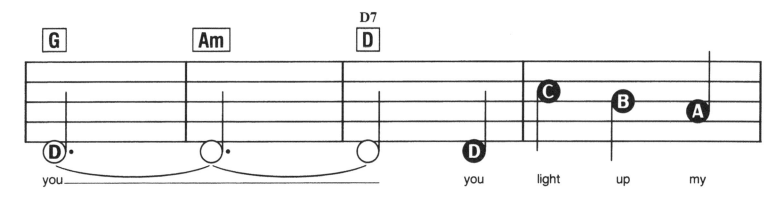

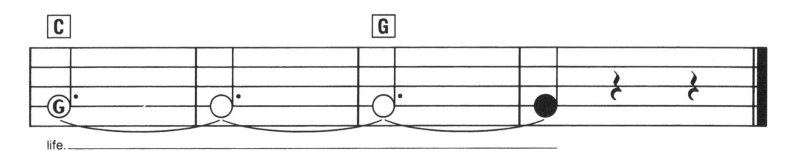

You Are So Beautiful

Registration 1
Rhythm: Pops or 8 Beat

Words and Music by Billy Preston
and Bruce Fisher

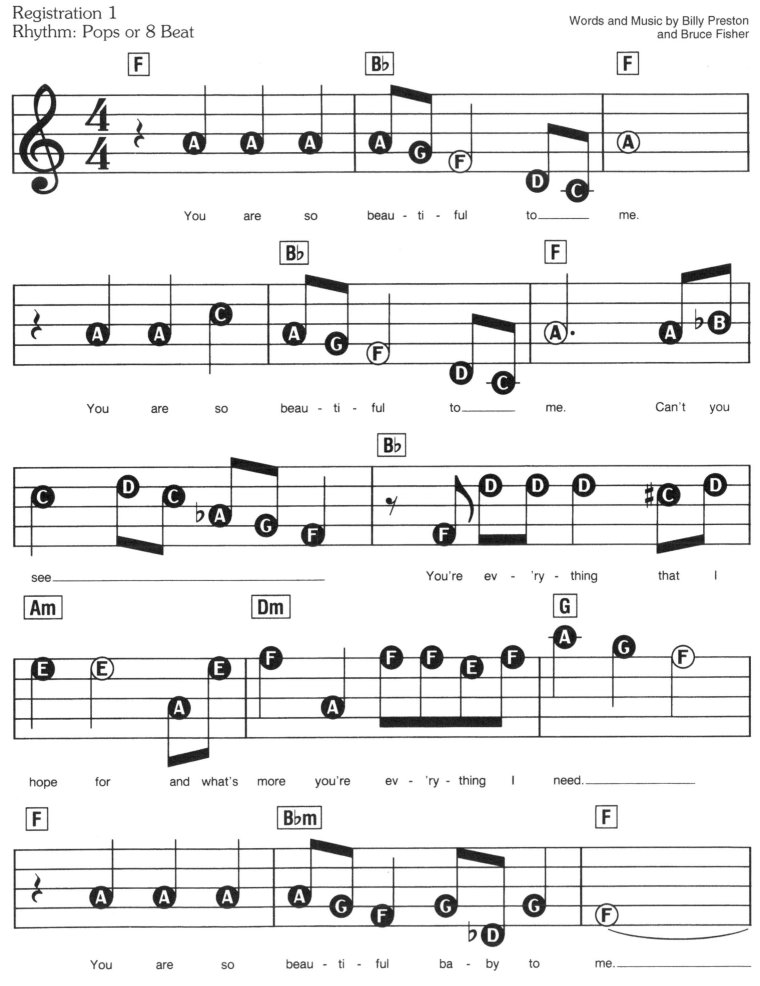

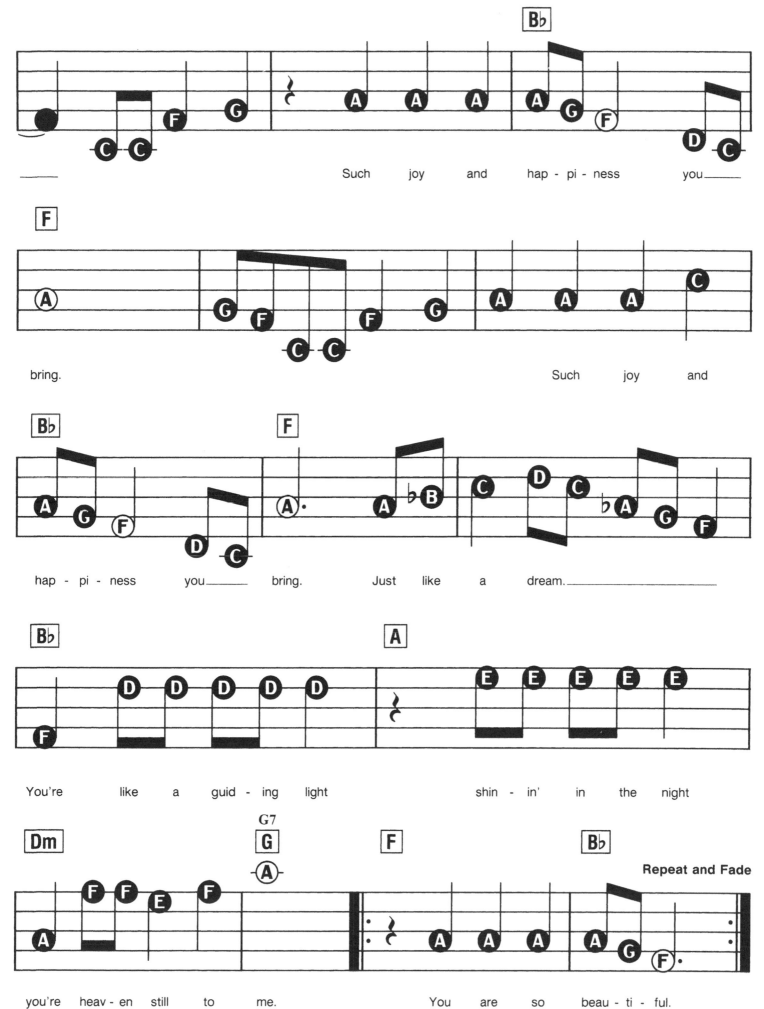

You Are the Sunshine of My Life

Registration 7
Rhythm: 8 Beat or Bossa Nova

Words and Music by
Stevie Wonder

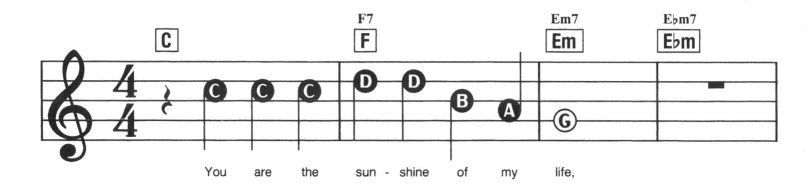

You are the sun - shine of my life,

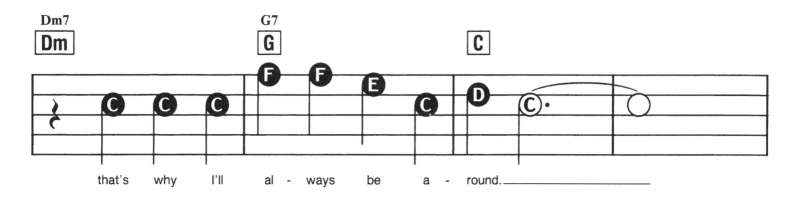

that's why I'll al - ways be a - round._____

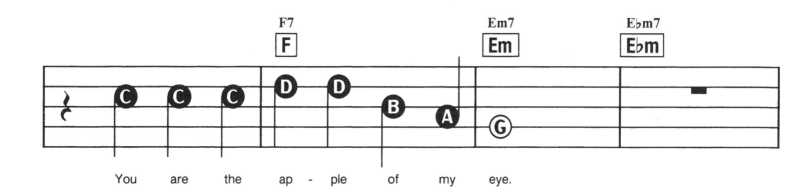

You are the ap - ple of my eye.

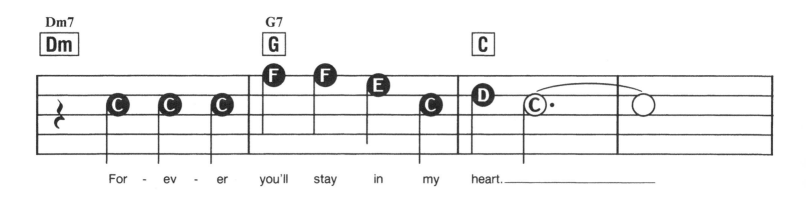

For - ev - er you'll stay in my heart._____

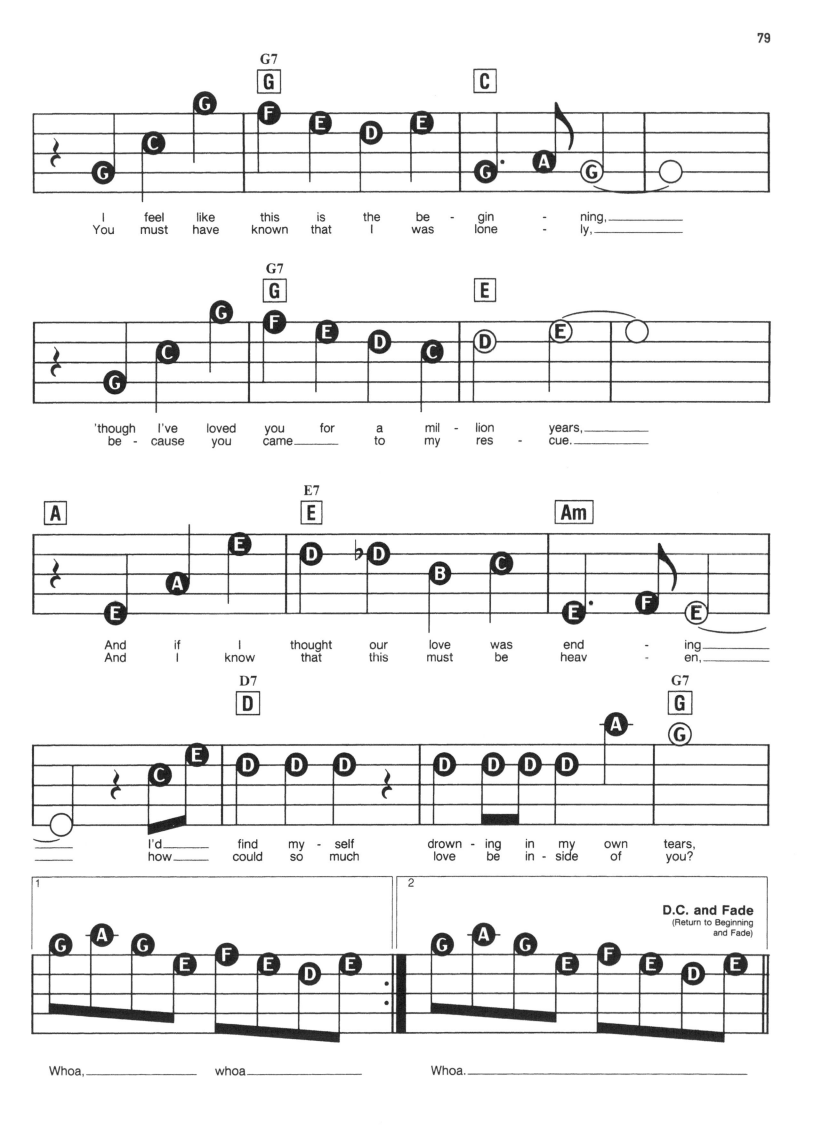

I feel like this is the be - gin - ning,_____
You must have known that I was lone - ly,_____

'though I've loved you for a mil - lion years,_____
be - cause you came_____ to my res - cue._____

And if I thought our love was end - ing_____
And I know that this love must be heav - en,_____

I'd_____ find my - self drown - ing in my own tears,
how_____ could so much love be in - side of you?

Whoa,_____ whoa_____ Whoa._____

D.C. and Fade
(Return to Beginning
and Fade)

Registration Guide

- Match the Registration number on the song to the corresponding numbered category below. Select and activate an instrumental sound available on your instrument.

- Choose an automatic rhythm appropriate to the mood and style of the song. (Consult your Owner's Guide for proper operation of automatic rhythm features.)

- Adjust the tempo and volume controls to comfortable settings.

Registration

1	Mellow	Flutes, Clarinet, Oboe, Flugel Horn, Trombone, French Horn, Organ Flutes
2	Ensemble	Brass Section, Sax Section, Wind Ensemble, Full Organ, Theater Organ
3	Strings	Violin, Viola, Cello, Fiddle, String Ensemble, Pizzicato, Organ Strings
4	Guitars	Acoustic/Electric Guitars, Banjo, Mandolin, Dulcimer, Ukulele, Hawaiian Guitar
5	Mallets	Vibraphone, Marimba, Xylophone, Steel Drums, Bells, Celesta, Chimes
6	Liturgical	Pipe Organ, Hand Bells, Vocal Ensemble, Choir, Organ Flutes
7	Bright	Saxophones, Trumpet, Mute Trumpet, Synth Leads, Jazz/Gospel Organs
8	Piano	Piano, Electric Piano, Honky Tonk Piano, Harpsichord, Clavi
9	Novelty	Melodic Percussion, Wah Trumpet, Synth, Whistle, Kazoo, Perc. Organ
10	Bellows	Accordion, French Accordion, Mussette, Harmonica, Pump Organ, Bagpipes